DR M   IR AND JOSIE SEY   L

Mindfulness
for Busy
People

Turning frantic and frazzled
into calm and composed

PEARSON

Harlow, England • London   apore • Hong Kong
Tokyo • Seoul • Taipei • N   nich • Paris • Milan

PEARSON EDUCATION LIMITED
Edinburgh Gate
Harlow CM20 2JE
United Kingdom
Tel: +44 (0)1279 623623
Web: www.pearson.com/uk

First published 2013 (print and electronic)

Pearson Education is not responsible for the content of third-party internet sites.

ISBN: 978-0-273-78990-1 (print)
       978-0-273-79461-5 (PDF)
       978-1-292-00848-6 (eText)
       978-0-273-79462-2 (ePub)

British Library Cataloguing-in-Publication Data
A catalogue record for the print edition is available from the British Library

Library of Congress Cataloging-in-Publication Data
Sinclair, Michael (Michael I.)
  Mindfulness for busy people : turning frantic and frazzled to calm and composed / Dr Michael Sinclair and Josie Seydel.
     pages cm
  Includes index.
  ISBN 978-0-273-78990-1 (pbk.) -- ISBN 978-0-273-79461-5 (PDF) -- ISBN 978-1-292-00848-6 (ePub)
  1. Mind and body. 2. Stress management. I. Seydel, Josie. II. Title.
  BF151.S56 2013
  155.9'042--dc23

                          2013027159

10 9 8 7 6 5
17 16 15 14

Cartoons by Stu McLellan
Cover design by Two Associates
Print edition typeset in 10/12pt ITC Giovanni Std by 30
Print edition printed and bound in Great Britain by Henry Ling Limited., at the Dorset Press, Dorchester, DT1 1HD

NOTE THAT ANY PAGE CROSS-REFERENCES REFER TO THE PRINT EDITION

Contents

About the authors

Dr Michael Sinclair and Josie Seydel have known each other since 2008 when their paths crossed professionally. Since this time they have spent endless hours yakking away and practising mindfulness together. They share a passion and zest for living life (despite how busy and stressful it can be) and sharing their experiences with one another. With their different backgrounds and journeys into the practice of mindfulness they are able to offer a unique collaborative insight into the experience of mindfulness practice. Both are also practising counselling psychologists with exceptional skills and experience.

Michael is a busy professional often juggling far too many things at once. At times he needs to be told when to slow down and take a rest. He has found that no matter what 'sh*t may be hitting the fan', mindfulness keeps him on track to deal with it all. His passion for psychology and mindfulness seems to know no bounds and he can bang on (and on!) about either topic if he's allowed to. He has been inspired in this boundless enthusiasm by the many amazing and resilient people he has met through his work as a practitioner psychologist over the past 14 years. He has worked with children, those suffering with life-threatening medical diagnoses and illnesses (and their loved ones), celebrities, top executives and many CEOs and senior business leaders. He has become fascinated by the shared humanity of experience, the common universal themes met in each of us and the human resilience to survive in the face of extreme adversity. Michael's tireless energy and commitment working as a successful consultant counselling psychologist, and as the clinical director of a thriving group practice in the City of London (City Psychology Group), has enabled him to help hundreds of people to discover and tap into this resilience, sense of shared humanity and wisdom, to cultivate these incredible qualities and to find a genuine sense of well-being. This is not least a personal endeavour, particularly since raising his three-year-old nephew following the recent and sudden death of his sister. Michael has also learnt that he can take off his superhero cape occasionally (although it does suit him very well), put his feet up and have a beer. As an associate fellow of the British Psychological Society (BPS) and a senior practitioner on the Register of Psychologists Specialising in Psychotherapy (BPS), Michael has also been trained in the USA by the pioneers of the mindfulness-based treatment approach, Acceptance and Commitment Therapy (ACT), and has taught mindfulness to hundreds of people over many years. He continues to provide the highest quality psychological therapy and coaching to people of all ages, couples, families and groups. He is the consultant to a number of corporate occupational health departments in the City of London, assisting with employees' stress management and productivity. He delivers cutting-edge mindfulness workshops to corporate managers, other health practitioners as well as larger public audiences. He is the author of self-help books and has also published academic papers on his research and practice. He is regularly sought after in the media as an expert in his field and is frequently interviewed for TV, newspapers and magazines. Michael has first-hand experience of the pressure and demands that we all face in this modern and busy world and he is continuously amazed by the beauty and simplicity of mindfulness in helping us to cope with it all.

Josie was first taught to meditate at the age of ten and remembers sitting in the car with her family silently reciting mantras. Given this experience it is not surprising that she chose to become a psychologist and continue to work on understanding what the heck that was all about. At the age of 18 Josie learned mindfulness meditation, hung out with hippies, travelled about and discovered that to find herself (wherever she was) she only needed to breathe. She became a chartered counselling psychologist in 2003 and is now also an associate fellow of the British Psychological Society. She has worked in several different and diverse settings during her career, including: specialist eating disorders services, refugee and asylum seeker services, domestic violence services, women's prisons, adolescent in-patient services and in primary schools. Everywhere she has gone she has found real human beings, from the highest corporate lawyers to the most dejected and shunned murderers, all also able to breathe and find themselves (with a little help) and to see that we are not so very different after all. She currently works as a clinical associate with City Psychology Group, in the City of London, providing mindfulness-based psychological therapy to people of all ages as well as pioneering mindfulness workshops to large public audiences. Josie is also the mother of two young children and so understands stress quite well. Through her compassionate and committed professional and personal dedication to practice she continues to marvel that mindfulness truly allows the heart to find ease. May you find this too.

Acknowledgements

'With deeply heartfelt gratitude to all our loved ones here and passed, and to those that we have ever had the pleasure to meet and serve in our work. You have touched us in so many ways; we remain enriched by our connection. May all your lives be filled with joy and blessings.'

Many thanks to Stu McLellan for his wonderful illustrations.

Introduction

You may have picked this book up because you are interested to learn more about mindfulness generally, what it can do for you and maybe how you could incorporate it into your busy life. Or you may simply be just so crazy busy right now and at your absolute wits end that you're willing to give anything a try (mindfulness or whatever it may take!) to find some relief and peace and quiet from your frantic existence. Either way, you've come to the right place – this book is for you.

> **"You've come to the right place – this book is for you."**

As busy people ourselves we know very well what it's like to be rushed off your feet, scrambling around, constantly on the go, never feeling like everything is done, that there is never enough time in the day, feeling tired, exhausted, stressed out and fed up most of the time … oh yes, we know this all too well. ('Hey, Michael did you remember to get back to all those very important people about all those very important things?' 'Well, I think so, but I'd better check …' 'Josie, did you send all those emails to everyone who ever existed?' 'Oh do you mean in that spare five minutes I had yesterday?' 'You had a spare five minutes?' 'Hang on – aren't we supposed to be doing something else right now, like writing a book?' 'Oops, oh yeah, there we go getting side-tracked again. Right, where were we? RE-FO-CUS!')

We also know what it's like when any moment of relaxation or satisfaction seems to never last quite long enough before the next stress comes along to blast any snippet of tranquillity away again! We understand how frustrating it is to be told to just slow down and relax, to just take some deep breaths and try to do less when you clearly, blinking very well can't (if only we had the time and it was all that easy)! Like you, we have heard all this from our caring friends and family members and also from the endless reams of Western psychology self-help books (many full of false promises), telling us to just think positively, to just take some time to simply switch off and relax, to delegate more to others and to get better at prioritising our daily tasks, oh and improving on our time management skills – yadda, yadda, yadda! Well, if like us you have tried all this then you've probably also found that it just doesn't work and it's just not that simple. If only when those times to relax do occur, they could just last a bit longer – ah, bliss!

We know that you are smart and intelligent, like us you have probably tried hard to figure all this out, to a find a way to be less stressed and busy in life – if it were just that easy and straightforward wouldn't we have figured this all out by now? So all this begs the question: what can we do when nothing that we do will do? Well, we have the answer, and we know that there isn't much else around to support and help us busy people to really manage all our busyness (or to do it well, anyway) – so for all these reasons we wanted to write this book. We know what it's like to be busy and we know what really can help – and that's something called (cue drum roll, please): *mindfulness*.

As practising psychologists in the City of London, we provide mindfulness-based therapy and coaching sessions and also run mindfulness and stress management workshops for very busy people just like you (and us), and we are keen to share some of the techniques and expert guidance that we use in our work with our clients and in our own personal lives every day; techniques that really do work straightaway to help you feel calm, confident and in more control of your busy day.

I have no time to waste, so is this book really for me?

There's no getting away from the fact that life is busy and there is no doubt so much else going on for you right now. So, it is great that you have chosen to dedicate some of your precious time and attention to checking this book out. We can assure you that if your life feels busy and overwhelming then picking up this book might well be the first step to a less stressful and more efficient and meaningful existence. This book was written with *you* in mind. We work with people just like you every day and know just how hard life can get; we also know mindfulness works because we use it every day, with our clients and in our own hectic lives. We have designed this book to meet the needs of those whose time is precious and who have precious little time. Many of the exercises are very brief and manageable, the content is designed to work for you 'on the go', in your life just as it is, and the cases included are relevant to common, modern-day stresses. We have included these case-examples (with names and identifying markers changed to respect confidentiality), directly from our work to outline how mindfulness can help to address some of the more common problems that our busy clients often come to see us about in our therapy room – such as burnout, tiredness, stress, physical aches and pains, anxiety and depression. We hope you will come to realise that these sorts of problems are common to all us busy people; we are all in the same boat here and we want to demonstrate how, just like it has helped our clients and us, *mindfulness* could help you too.

> ❝ *We have designed this book to meet the needs of those whose time is precious and who have precious little time.* ❞

With all this said, we wouldn't want you to just take our word for it or waste any more of your valuable time so we thought we'd get you to ask yourself a few questions straight away to help you decide for yourself if you want to read on. Have a read through the following questions – would you answer 'yes' to any of them?

- ▶ Does your day 'run away with you' leaving you little or no time to do what you really want to do?
- ▶ Do you feel that if one more thing goes wrong then you're likely to explode?
- ▶ Are you constantly trying to juggle more than one thing at a time?
- ▶ Do you find that your time and attention is being pulled in every which way possible?
- ▶ Can you feel stressed out, anxious or irritated?
- ▶ Are you amazed by how much you get done but never feel that you are completely able to just stop and relax?
- ▶ Can your mood become sad or flat for no apparent reason?
- ▶ Do you find it hard to concentrate or focus at times?
- ▶ Do you often dream of a different life, free from stress and constant demands?
- ▶ Can you become snappy or short with friends or loved ones?
- ▶ Do you feel bored, demotivated, inefficient, unproductive or lacking in creativity at times, in one or more aspects of life?
- ▶ Do you find that you can get carried away by your thoughts or that your thoughts are often stressful?
- ▶ Can you find it hard to fall and/or stay asleep?
- ▶ Can you suddenly feel exhausted and tired?
- ▶ Do you feel that everyone around you demands your time and attention?
- ▶ Do you suffer from any physical aches and pains?
- ▶ Do you tend to comfort eat, use alcohol or drugs to ease your stress?

If you answered 'yes' to any one (or all!) of these questions then we encourage you to keep reading.

This book will introduce you to the life-changing practice of mindfulness, helping you to de-stress, find your own unique space of calm and ready yourself for whatever challenges (good or bad) your busy life may bring your way. There is a pool of tranquillity lying just beneath the surface of your busy existence and this book will show you how to take a dip into that pool whenever you choose. It will demonstrate to you how you can become more efficient and effective and make the most out of the precious, limited time that you have. Moreover, if you are looking at this book and wondering what this 'mindfulness-thing' that everyone has been talking about actually is, want to learn what it can do for you and maybe even try it out (if only you had the time!), then this book is certainly for you. If you then chose to practise mindfulness regularly then let us warn you – it *will* change your life (in a good way). You can expect to manage your stress and busyness both at home and at work with much more ease and efficiency.

Specifically, by practising mindfulness regularly you can expect to:

- Feel happier and more contented.
- Improve your motivation and energy levels.
- Be more productive and effective.
- Improve your mental and physical stamina
- Boost your immune system and improve your general health
- Decrease your stress and chances of other mental health problems.
- Improve your memory and concentration and increase your brain-wave activity.
- Enhance your intuition and creativity.
- Enhance your communication skills and enjoy more fulfilling relationships.
- Create a more enjoyable, meaningful and fulfilling life.

All sounds good, huh? Well, we're not here to sell you false promises; all these benefits are yours for the taking. You will, however, need to practise mindfulness to notice them happening for you – and we are going to show you just how to do this throughout this book, without the need to find any extra time in your busy day.

What we'll cover in this book and how to use it

In this book, we are keen to:

▶ Show you how mindfulness can dramatically improve your busy life.

▶ Teach you some ways to practise it that are especially easy to fit into your busy life.

▶ Illustrate to you just how accessible, infinite and abundantly present mindfulness actually already is to you, despite how busy you are.

▶ Show how you can use quick and easy techniques to tap into it without changing anything around you and your circumstances at all.

▶ Show you how to cultivate less stress and more well-being and efficiency in any given moment of your busy life.

You will not need to shave your head, wear a saffron robe and eat lentils on a mountain-top to practise mindfulness, but you will need to keep an open and curious mind to trying something in a completely new way – such as brushing your teeth mindfully (yes, we really mean it).

We've written this book specifically for you because being so busy probably means that you don't have the time to read most of the other mindfulness books that may be rooted in more spiritual teachings and/ or offer you lengthier programmes to follow over a number of weeks. So we have designed this book as a kind of guide to mindfulness-on-the-go. Other books on the topic may invite you to sit cross-legged meditating for hours on end (and of course you can if you choose to), but we're of the belief that you don't have to do this to practise mindfulness and reap the benefits of it.

The real mindfulness practice is how we live our lives, moment to moment, day to day. Let's face it our lives are pretty busy in these modern times. We don't have to change our modern world to fit in with mindfulness practice, but we can change our practice to fit in with our modern world. The beauty is that mindfulness actually creates space and when it feels like you are suffocating under piles of stuff to get done, it's really a great ally to have. So don't think of it as yet another futile time-consumer, you'll soon see how it's actually an effective time saver.

" The more mindfulness practice you do,
the more you will feel the benefit. "

We want to provide you with a more succinct, accessible and practical approach to cultivating mindfulness in your life, so hopefully you feel able and willing to integrate it with your busy life just as it is. Whether you choose to spend more or less time on your mindfulness practice, either is absolutely fine – although the more mindfulness practice you do, the more you will feel the benefit.

This book is full of practical mindfulness exercises, designed to fit into your busy life as it is. For quick reference and easy accessibility you'll find them dotted throughout the book, under the heading **I haven't got time for this practice**.

You'll also find other features dotted around the book for quick and easy reference. These are other types of exercises that are to be used whenever you like (as much as you like) and you'll find these under the heading **Mindfulness on-the-go**.

You'll also notice that we have included some quizzes and mini exercises here and there, which are designed to get you thinking and reflecting on the principles of mindfulness. You'll notice these are under the heading **Mindfulness reflection moment**.

Finally, we've summarised salient learning points at the end of each chapter for you, these are under the heading **Mindfulness top tips to-go**.

As you read through the book, you will be invited to try out these practices and exercises for yourself, to have a go at some quizzes and reflect on the principles being taught.

Audio recordings are also included, which will assist you as a guide through certain exercises (should you want to use them), they are indicated by this symbol:

Why is this book full of practical exercises you may ask? Well, we can tell you all about mindfulness and you can appreciate, understand and grasp it – but unless you do it, it won't make the slightest difference to your life! Rather than only taking our word on this, here's what the late Steve Jobs had to say on the subject:

'If you just sit and observe, you will see how restless your mind is,' Jobs told his biographer, Walter Isaacson. 'If you try to calm it, it only makes it worse, but over time it does calm, and when it does, there's room to hear more subtle things – that's when your intuition starts to blossom and you start to see things more clearly and be in the present more. Your mind just slows down, and you see a tremendous expanse in the moment. You see so much more than you could see before. *It's a discipline; you have to practise it.'*

Steve Jobs – co-founder, chairman and CEO of Apple Inc.

Please try not to rush through this book. If you have the urge to skip forward, which is understandable (for whatever reason), just become aware of that urge and then let it pass by as it will naturally (you'll understand what we mean by this soon enough), as you continue to stay focused on what you are reading in that moment. The answers to some of our problems will not always be found where we assume them to be, they might actually be in the *awareness* that you have right here and now!

Part 1

Mindfulness and me

What is this all about and how's it going to help me?

In this first section of the book we are keen to:

- ▷ Introduce you to mindfulness, its origins and uses.
- ▷ Explain what mindfulness is all about.
- ▷ Help you get a better understanding of why and how it can be relevant and helpful to us all in these stressful and busy modern times.
- ▷ Show you how to start practising mindfulness.

How can mindfulness change your life?

In this chapter we're going to show you:

▶ How you don't need to change your life to practise or benefit from mindfulness.

▶ Briefly, what mindfulness is all about – and what it isn't about.

▶ What the many benefits of mindfulness actually are, including what the research tells us; such as how it changes the brain (in a good way). (Yes, we are geeks, and we think that you'll probably love this stuff too. If not please be patient with us as you read through it – we just couldn't leave it out.)

So, how can mindfulness change your life? Well, firstly let's clear something up. It might be that your life doesn't change at all (stay with us now). This doesn't mean it will not become radically different. Confused? Well listen to this:

> Two similar objects appear different because of the difference in the mind that perceives them.
>
> **Patanjali, Yoga sutras, 2nd century BCE, verse 15, 'Enlightenment', in translation by Centre for Inner Peace**

Nothing external to our own minds need be any different, no person, situation or environment, or even thoughts about these, needs to change in order for us to experience and react to our busy lives in a radically different way. Or let's put it another way … there is a daisy growing in your lawn, to Billy it is beautiful, but Bertie thinks it is a weed. Billy feels full of divine love, Bertie gets the hump. Contrary to popular Western psychology, and still as relevant today as it was back in 2nd century BCE India, we need to change nothing, we need to do nothing other than foster *acceptance* of what is (to be less busy and more efficient), and mindfulness is a wonderful tool for enhancing the likelihood of this happening.

> "*We need to change nothing, we need to do nothing other than foster* acceptance *of what is.*"

Stress and other emotional disturbances, actually arise from our thoughts and reactions to our busy lives, rather than from our busy lives themselves. Again, let's put this another way: Billy feels love, not because of the daisy itself, but because of his *thoughts about* the daisy; Bertie feels annoyed, not because of the daisy, but because of his *thoughts about* the daisy. Using mindfulness it is possible to acknowledge these thoughts and any other emotions and experiences that we have, and stand back from them. We can then untangle ourselves from them, free ourselves from an attachment to them as how things 'once were' in the past or 'ought to be' in the future and instead see them as they are right now. Mindfulness makes no demands that we 'change', that life has to be different in any way, but rather works on a basis of acceptance, in a radical sense, of the present moment.

Acceptance does not mean giving up or being lazy

A common concern (please see the **Mindfulness is NOT...** section later on in this chapter for other common concerns) that we hear from very busy and achieving people is that they will become lazy or complacent – never meeting deadlines, shortening their to-do lists or making changes to the important aspects of their life – if they just simply accept everything how it is. Well, nothing could be further from the truth: to limit stress and busyness in life, to become more effective and productive, it is important to move on the things that we can change and let go of the struggle to change the things that we can't. From acceptance often comes clarity of mind and with that arises the possibility of change to help us get ahead in life.

So, developing acceptance does not mean that we might not wish to do anything to resolve difficulties and are a passive passenger to the whims of our life's meanderings. It does mean that we develop a true freedom from our habitual and often distressing tendency to *react* to life without reflection, to hold fast to notions of something *having* to be different and instead reveal the liberating gift of our own creative, loving and present mind. We become free to be part of our life here and now. Check out this quote:

> Radical Acceptance reverses our habit of living at war with experiences that are unfamiliar, frightening or intense. It is the necessary antidote to years of neglecting ourselves, years of judging ourselves and treating ourselves harshly, years of rejecting the moment's experience. Radical acceptance is the willingness to experience ourselves and our life as it is. A moment of radical acceptance is a moment of genuine freedom.
>
> *Radical Acceptance*, Tara Brach, 2003

Holy smoke! Amazing! Genuine freedom! This is pretty full on though, isn't it? Are you ready to let go of fear, sorrow, pain and anger – and what about busyness? Well, truly you can. But don't worry, this is not very easy to do, so you have plenty of time to practise with mindfulness and a wonderful journey of exploration to begin. Before you set off, please forget to pack, leave your passport in the drawer and stay seated. In other words: 'don't do something, just sit there'; all this journey requires is for you to be present, where you are, right now.

Mindfulness has already changed many lives

Mindfulness has been introduced to the Western world over the past several decades, not just by hippies hoping to become all 'Zen baby', but also in medical, health, family and business settings. For example, Jon Kabat-Zinn, who has written many books (see the section **Recommended reading**), has done some fabulous work using mindfulness as part of a stress-reduction programme in Massachusetts. This programme began in the late 1970s, to help lots of people manage their stress, anxiety, pain and illness. He writes this:

> Most people come to the clinic because they want to relax. But they often leave transformed beyond anything they hoped to accomplish in the first place ... None of these 'results' was predictable. But they all grew directly out of the meditation [mindfulness] practice.

> Jon Kabat-Zinn

In our own clinical practice as psychologists we have seen and taught mindfulness to many busy professionals feeling overwhelmed with life, stressed or burnt out and many people in general with a vast range of difficulties, of all ages and backgrounds, people like you, people like us. The benefits of practising mindfulness for these people have been really, quite astonishing.

Scientifically supported

You don't just have to take our word for this ... (Yes, you guessed it; here comes the geeky stuff, what gave it away? The title up there we presume. So brace yourself, you know you want to hear it really too.)

Over the past few decades, more and more scientific research has been conducted to investigate the effects of mindfulness practice on our brains, minds, emotions, behaviours, functioning and bodies. This research is showing us how mindfulness can effectively help many difficulties such as depression, anxiety, stress, psychosis, body image problems, abuse, trauma, eating disorders, ADHD, nicotine addiction, attention and memory problems, low self-esteem, work-related stress, psoriasis, acute and chronic pain, relationship problems and parenting teenagers and children. There is potentially so much to say on each of these topics that we, your beloved authors, find ourselves lost in fantasising about more books, perhaps our own TV show (the fame, the glory – oh darlings!). However, we are able to let go of that, using our mindful awareness of now – seeing this moment as it simply is and daring to be simple with it. The temptation to be pulled away from now into something more pressing, important, urgent, different or just 'not this' is very compelling. But, as we will see, this is just an engaging story, which serves only to take us out of our lives and away from ourselves and others. It is inefficient right now. No wonder life loses its flavour. Whether this loss of flavour is branded as stress, ADHD, chronic pain, glory-seeking or something else, the struggle, the real 'problem' is in the pushing away of *life*, of now. We do this just like you do. We know this and, perhaps unlike you (at this moment), we know and are going to help you to know too that this can be different.

Research has also shown how mindfulness practice can actually change areas of the brain associated with improved cognitive functioning and the ability to regulate emotions. In one study, after only 11 hours of mindfulness practice structural changes were observed in participants' brains around the anterior cingulate cortex, a part of the brain involved in monitoring our focus and self-control. In another study, participants had brain scans before and after an eight-week mindfulness-based stress-reduction programme. Compared to people who had not done the programme, researchers found increases in key areas of the brain associated with learning and memory processes as well as the ability to take on different perspectives. Since we all use our learning and memory regularly, whether it is remembering the keys on the way to work, ensuring that you remember to pick up the kids from school or learning to use a new computer system, research demonstrates the effectiveness of using mindfulness to aid these vital brain processes.

Have you ever experienced difficulties concentrating or paying attention (or is that just us)? Have you ever experienced difficulties concentrating or paying attention (or is that just us)? Have you ever experienced … (ha ha ha). More nerdy research 'factoids' tells us that our attention can be improved using mindfulness, helping to improve focus and avoid distractions. It could also help us with our communication skills, helping us hold back from knee-jerk negative reactions, improving our social connectedness and relationships, which are crucial for human survival and general well-being.

We all experience stress within our everyday lives, from upcoming, pressing deadlines or managing a busy household, and at times we may feel overwhelmed. Mindfulness researchers have shown that those who practise mindfulness tend to use more helpful coping strategies when in stressful situations, helping them to be more productive with their time. And even when your stress comes from something as scary as cancer, mindfulness has been shown to help people manage and reduce their stress levels in the face of this effectively too.

So, why do we experience improved well-being after being 'mindful'? Well, further neurobiological changes within the brain may provide this explanation. Using brain imaging techniques, neuroscientists have observed changes in the 'threat system' of the brain following mindfulness practice. Studies have found that an eight-week mindfulness course reduces the reactivity and the density of neurons in the amygdala (the part of the brain associated with the 'fight or flight response' and which triggers fear) and increased activity in areas of the prefrontal cortex that help regulate emotions, subsequently reducing stress. Other research into the brain's electrical signals has shown that ongoing mindfulness practice was associated with increased alpha wave activity, linked to relaxation and decreased anxiety. Using brain scan technology, scientists have also shown that structural changes occur in the brain after mindfulness practice, with more connections between different areas of the brain and an increase in a protective nerve tissue called myelin, essential for healthy brain function.

> "Scientists have also shown that structural changes
> occur in the brain after mindfulness practice."

So mindfulness helps us to manage our moods and stress levels and this is not just because we are being still for a second, stuff is actually happening in the brain (how awesome is that?) – check out this quote:

Changes in brain structure may underlie some of these reported improvements and that people are not just feeling better because they are spending time relaxing.

Sara Lazar, PhD, of the MGH Psychiatric Neuroimaging Research Program

Not only does the use of mindfulness have benefits for our minds, but there has also been growing evidence supporting the use of mindfulness for improved immune system functioning and better physical health. Illness is something we all try to avoid and mindfulness may help you do just that. Research has shown that even after eight weeks of mindfulness practice, people had changes in immune functioning with a greater antibody count. Mindfulness practice can also help you manage pain more effectively without the aid of painkillers. After a period of mindfulness practice, participants in research studies report lower pain intensity experiences, both in the laboratory and in real-life chronic conditions such as arthritis and back and neck pain.

And as we have said, it is not just in a clinical setting that mindfulness has been proven extraordinarily advantageous and profitable. It is also proven helpful with general sleep problems, weight management, stopping smoking and can also dramatically improve focus, attention, concentration, creativity and performance in business, sports and exercise, as well as bringing more satisfaction to many areas of our daily activities such as work and our relationships with friends, colleagues and loved ones.

Impressive stuff – but does all this really matter? We've enjoyed indulging our geeky side, which has given us the opportunity to feel like we are doing our very best at getting you to buy into all this some more – but again, does it really matter? No point reading about it and how amazing the research findings are, as Nike says – 'just do it' for yourself and you'll become your very own science project, and able to write up your own research findings, if you like.

Mindfulness actually originates from ancient Eastern philosophies but has more recently become a very hot topic in Western psychology. Currently (and understandably when you consider all the benefits outlined above), there is a lot of excitement and activity around mindfulness in the scientific community and research has proven that mindfulness can dramatically improve our well-being and performance in many areas of our modern and busy lives. If you want to know more and find out how you can start to benefit from mindfulness yourself, then please read on and use this book as a guide to show you how you can start practising it for yourself, throughout your busy life.

The benefits of mindfulness for a busy life (in a nutshell)

Mindfulness allows us to notice how we are responding to any given moment, including the stressful times that we experience throughout our life, showing us how to not exacerbate painful moments and to truly savour the pleasant ones if we choose to. It provides us with the vital space within which we can stand firm and strong when our busy lives feel stressful and overwhelming. It reminds us that our sense of peace and stability is where it has always been, internal to us, residing right here and now inside of us all despite our external life circumstances; it teaches us how to touch base with this already existing unique place of peace and stillness, and to cultivate and strengthen it amidst this frantic and increasingly pressured world in which we live.

Mindfulness is quite contrary to our tendency to live on *autopilot* (more about this in Part 2). As a new and more meaningful modus operandi, mindfulness helps us:

▶ to de-stress and relax;

▶ to build resilience in the face of inevitable daily stress;

▶ to free up our creativity, improve our performance, and efficiency;

▶ to tap into our natural source of physical and mental energy; and

▶ to truly create the effective, efficient, meaningful and fun reality that we want for ourselves.

If all this sounds good to you, and you'd like to do some of this mindfulness stuff, then do read on.

Mindfulness is NOT...

Before you get cracking, at this preliminary stage we also quickly wanted to dispel some common untruths and myths about mindfulness (we know we still battle with letting go of some of these at times, even after years of our own personal practice). We hope that this will encourage you to continue reading as well as begin to gain a better understanding of what is to follow on your journey through this book and your practice. The following explanations are designed to get straight to the point, so don't worry if anything feels unclear at this stage, it will all be covered and explained further as you continue reading and start to practise yourself.

... meditation

Contrary to popular assumptions and belief mindfulness is NOT a meditation. Meditation is simply a way to practise, cultivate and reinforce the principles of mindfulness as a way of being, which is all about kindness, curiosity, compassion and acceptance towards yourself and your experience and the world around you. The real meditation is how you carry yourself in any given moment throughout your busy life in all its various contexts, wherever you are, whatever you may be doing, whatever role you may be in and whoever you may be with. Mindfulness is very relevant to us all and we want to show you how it can be incorporated into all aspects of our busy lives. We promise, you won't have to join a temple, sit cross-legged in the lotus position or chant to monotone sounds for hours on end to practise mindfulness nor to reap the many rewards that it has to offer your life.

... subject to time constraints

A common excuse that we hear from many of our busy clients is that they simply don't have the time to practise mindfulness. Well, they have since discovered as you will too, that nothing could be further from the truth and this is exactly what this book is all about! Mindfulness is abundant and infinite, it is there with you in every moment in which you live, it is with you right now as you read the pages of this book, there is ample time and opportunity to practise mindfulness in any moment of your life and therefore there is no excuse! It is often best practised during activities that you would usually do habitually, on autopilot mode – such as checking and sending emails on your smartphone, getting dressed, brushing your teeth, taking a shower, standing in a queue, waiting for a train, etc. – so we are certain that you'll have lots of opportunities to practise it without necessarily escaping to a Buddhist retreat somewhere far, far away. It's all about making a *virtue out of a necessity* and we're keen to show you just how.

Mindfulness is abundant and infinite, it is there with you in every moment in which you live.

... dependent on surroundings

As we said above, people often say that they are too busy, have too much going on or are surrounded by too many noisy and demanding people either in the office or at home, for them to take themselves away to find a quiet place to practise mindfulness. Again, when we hear this, we just tend to hear excuses and habitual patterns of the mind (more about this in Part 2). It may surprise you to know that we actually have a lot to be mindful of while surrounded by our noisy or demanding environments. We're going to show you just how lucky you actually are and how much opportunity you actually have to be able to practise mindfulness amidst your busy and stressful life just as it is.

... relaxation

Although mindfulness practice will no doubt bring a deeper sense of relaxation and calmness (along with other improvements to your levels of functioning, performing, productivity and creativity in general), it is very important to remember that all these are simply fortunate and welcomed by-products of practising mindfulness. Relaxation and the other improvements listed above are not the goal of mindfulness practice (they may arise as an outcome if we lessen our preoccupation with them), the goal is to cultivate awareness and a new way of carrying yourself through your busy life – with this intention and goal in mind, along with an attitude of indifference and casualness as to whether or not you experience more relaxation and any other lucky by-products of practice as an outcome, you will be sure to reap these aforementioned rewards sooner.

... losing control, escaping reality, going into a trance, becoming complacent and navel-gazing

This is a very common early misconception that we hear often from our high-achieving and busy clients. In fact nothing could be further from the truth – mindfulness is the complete opposite of this assumption. Mindfulness is all about facing reality head-on and becoming more connected with your life experience. With practice you will become more attuned to yourself and the world around you. You will be more conscious to your emotional changeability and you will start to understand yourself with accuracy and clarity, feeling more in control of yourself and your actions. You will come to accept your experience just how it is in reality and cope with what you feel in any given moment. An array of alternative options and ideas will then open up for you, for you to choose to move on, ensuring that you have the best opportunity to act in your interest and move forward and achieve what you want in any context of your life.

... selfish and lazy

Many of us feel that we would be selfish or lazy if we spend time on practices for self-development. We believe that we simply can't look after ourselves until everyone else and everything else is attended to first. Well again nothing could be further from the truth on both accounts. First, mindfulness takes effort and a lot of discipline (there's nothing lazy about it) – it's about cultivating the most profound paradigm shift in our way of being that is known to mankind, and that certainly isn't easy. Years and even centuries of reinforced habits (going back to the days of our cave-dwelling ancestors; see Part 2 of this book to learn a bit more about this) are being observed and undone with each practice. Second, and further to all this, if we believe that we can't take time out for ourselves to help us cope better and de-stress until everything else is attended to first (which will never actually be achieved), then it would be fair to say that we run the risk of burnout, leaving us totally immobilised to give any more of ourselves, our time, our attention and our energy to others and the work and relationships that we consider important to us. Selfishness and laziness (should they arise for you) are both experiences to be observed within mindfulness practice and the very act of observing them leaves us with the choice of whether or not we want to act on them.

... clearing your mind of thoughts

This is a common incorrect assumption that captures the very essence of what mindfulness is all about. Mindfulness is all about acceptance of what is, what occurs naturally with no preference for something else. There is no agenda of clearing thoughts from your mind, but just awareness of what thoughts are there should they show up in your mind at any given moment. If you try to clear your mind of thoughts you will soon know about it because you will become immediately frustrated

– it's impossible! Distraction by our thoughts is inevitable within mind-fulness practice and not a sign of failure. It is impossible to clear our mind of thoughts, but what is possible is awareness of our thoughts and practising this very act through mindfulness will lead to less thoughts showing up and getting in the way of what you really want to do there-after (check out Part 2 of this book to discover more about practising mindfulness of thoughts).

... a quick fix to all my problems

Although you will no doubt experience the benefits of mindfulness straight away, as soon as you start practising it, it is by no means a guar-antee to get rid of or cure the undesirable experiences in life (if that were possible, we promise, we'd definitely be writing about that now instead). Mindfulness is to be cultivated and grown as a way of being, over time – there is no agenda (apart from cultivating more awareness of your experience), no end goal or result but instead welcomed and helpful by-products of regular practice along the way. Your emotional experience is varied as is the ever-changing world that exists around you – mindfulness is here to help you cope with all that. The very practice of mindfulness may bring with it frustration, disappointment, discourage-ment, stress, despondence and even anxiety. It is all about awareness and acceptance of our experience from which you will come to experience less frequent and intense episodes of undesirable feelings, simply as a welcomed by-product.

Making a virtue out of necessity

We hope that by now we have made it clear to you how mindfulness can 'change your life'. Just in case, we wanted to summarise the benefits of mindfulness for us busy people in these modern times in three clear points. No matter how busy and stressful your life may be, mindfulness will bring you:

1 Improved resilience, well-being, functioning and efficiency.
2 Less stress, less busyness and more peace and calmness.
3 A greater sense of meaning, satisfaction and enjoyment in life.

As we have said, with this book as your guide, you'll have ample oppor-tunity to practise mindfulness throughout your every day. You won't have to jump on a flight to a faraway mystical land, nor will you have to carve out extra time in your day to practise on top of everything else that you have to fit in and do (however, if you wanted to do either of these things that would be OK too). The beauty is that you can incorporate mindfulness into your everyday activities. Now, this doesn't mean that you can carry on aimlessly about your busyness and benefit from all that mindfulness has to offer you. You will have to bring a *purposeful intention of openness, acceptance and curiosity* to your everyday experiences, to incorporate mindfulness into whatever you may be doing. Sounds simple, hey? Well it is. It is very simple to be less busy and stressed and more productive but it is difficult to be simple. Are you willing to give it a go? Do you dare to be extraordinary? You need to practise mindfulness within your everyday tasks but in doing so we assure you that these mundane, everyday tasks will never feel the same again. Your eyes will open with amazement to the beauty of your life unfolding; you will notice what you have never noticed before and take more enjoyment from things that you thought would be impossible to enjoy.

> ❝ *It is very simple to be less busy and stressed and more productive but it is difficult to be simple.* ❞

Mindfulness top tips to-go

In this chapter you have understood that:

▶ You don't need to change your life or any of its circumstances to practise and benefit from mindfulness.

▶ We are all in the same boat, busy *doing* a lot of the time, more aligned with the term *human-doing* than *human-being* (more on this to follow soon).

▶ There are many unhelpful 'myths' that get in the way of practising mindfulness.

▶ You have to make a purposeful effort to practise mindfulness.

▶ Mindfulness can bring benefit to so many of our difficulties.

▶ Mindfulness can dramatically improve your busy life.

2

Busy much?!

In this chapter you will begin to discover:

▶ What type of busy person you really are.

▶ What it actually is that keeps you busy in your life.

▶ The secret to multitasking and being more efficient and effective.

Let's accept it, as there really is no getting away from it; we live in a busy, frantic and stressful world. Not only are we bombarded by daily and even 'moment-to-moment' demands on our time and attention, but we are also obsessed with the pursuit of happiness and high achievement, risking dangerous stress levels, meltdown or much worse.

❝ *The truth is that busyness and stress are inevitable parts of our lives.* ❞

The truth is that busyness and stress are inevitable parts of our lives, and especially for those of us that live in these modern times amidst ever-increasing advancements in technology and more and more pressure to perform at peak levels in all areas of life, all around the clock! There seems to be a great paradox that has arisen in our modern society. The more we invent smarter and faster ways of getting things done the more we are actually creating a frightening world of information overload and are also caging ourselves in increasing levels of stress (that we just want to escape from most of the time). We are overwhelmed by daily demands and pressures, shooting off emails here and there, checking and responding to others on our social networking profiles, ensuring that we are kept in the loop while also not ignoring others, working harder and longer to keep our jobs during these unpredictable times, including when we are not even physically present in the office (because if we don't someone else will be sure to beat us off the mark), helping friends, family and the postman's cat with all manner of problems, and generally spending much of our time rushing from one task to the next, trying to get everything done, attended to and ticked off of our to-do list. Phew! That was a lot to get condensed in one sentence and there surely is even more to get done in reality.

Now on top of that daily grind, there are still the inevitable traumatic incidents and derailing upheavals to deal with that life throws at us from time to time. These events tend to come without much warning, out of the blue and unexpected, and many of them can prove to be life-changing and challenging to cope with, such as the illness or death of a loved one, an acute or chronic physical injury or illness of our own, a relationship ending, a sudden redundancy or even a house fire or car theft, to name just a few common possibilities. In the absence of such eventualities, we seem to forget to leave any room for them as we go about our daily routines and meeting all the demands we face, filling up our days – which are often already busting at the seams – with more and more stuff. It's as if most of us are walking along a very fine tightrope indeed, about to lose our balance with the next unforeseen pressure flying at us from any angle out of the blue, and then we fall, crashing to the ground at any given moment. Sound familiar?

As if all this wasn't enough to contend with, along the way we also seem preoccupied with achievement and securing success in nearly all aspects of life while also searching for some peace, relaxation and happiness via whatever means (including ticking off the items on our never ending to-do list) as if such a time and state could be reached and anchored indefinitely. The more we strive for this illusion it is understandable that we will inevitably become more stressed, anxious, depressed and burnt out. If we really take a look at the pressure we put ourselves under and all that we are expected to cope with it would seem that most of us think we are superhuman and would presume to find ourselves among others in the DC Comic's superheroes' hall of fame. Have a go at thinking through the exercise below to check out what Busy Superhero you might be trying to be.

Exercise 2.1: Mindfulness reflection moment

What Busy Superhero am I?

See if you can recognise your busy self among any of these Busy Superhero profiles. Once you have read through them, have a think about which you are most like.

Work-O-Holic – saving the world with a spreadsheet!

Work-O-Holic is busy with work, racing against the clock and trying to rid the world of unrelenting workloads, crowded and cluttered email inboxes, general disorganisation, messy and abstract agendas and failing projects. Using certain secret superpowers and tools such as his/her acute and pedantic attention to detail, skilful planning, organisational and procedural prowess and trusty spreadsheets and the invincible power to run millions of to-do lists at once, Work-O-Holic is tirelessly rushing from one work task to the next, zapping piles of paperwork, disorder and the potential for global failure where it really hurts!

Captain Do-Good – saving the world with a cupcake!

Do-Good is busy pleasing others, taking on tasks for everyone that may (or not!) need some help, trying to rid the world of others' unhappiness and pain. With a steady flow of cupcakes baking in the oven, a spectacular collection of miraculous cleaning products at hand, extra booster seats for the school run and superhuman solutions for all – oh, and a bionic sympathetic listening device to boot – he/she is set to relieve others of discomfort and ensure that they always have someone to rely on forever, come rain or shine! No one will ever feel unwanted or neglected again with Captain Do-Good protecting the planet!

The Fox – saving the world with a treadmill!

The Fox is busy with working out in the gym and spinning classes a lot of the time, trying to rid the world of ugliness and physical imperfections. With a rolling gold-plus gym membership, A-list celebrity photos to hand, a full library of bulletproof diets, a trusty plastic surgeon on speed-dial and super-reflective fold out portable mirrors, The Fox feels well equipped to win the fight against ageing and ensure global physical perfection once and for all!

Dr Cure-All – saving the world with a blood pressure monitor!

Dr Cure-All is busy checking on health, trying to rid the world of disease and death. With supercharged blood pressure monitors, unbreakable mercury-filled thermometers, batches of super-foods and multi super-vitamins at the ready and a broadband connection faster than the speed of light to ensure a direct link to doctors online, Dr Cure-All is on a single minded mission to eradicate all death, physical illness, weakness, aches and pains!

Saccharinnia/Saccharissimo – saving the world with a Mills and Boon novel!

Saccharinnia/Saccharissimo is busy radiating sparkling love and honey-moon romance for all to enjoy, trying to rid the world of relationship imperfections and boring, unsatisfying and failed marriages. With a supernatural and invincible perception for a partner's flaws and annoy-ances, a rolling subscription to *Hello* magazine and the full series of Mills and Boon novels to hand, he/she is relentlessly creating a world where no one ever feels trapped in uncomfortable relationships and tramples on all potential relationship regrets.

Like most of us you may have found similarities between bits of yourself and more than one of these Busy Superheroes (if not, perhaps you'd like to make one up for yourself?). That's OK and really quite normal; we can all become preoccupied with trying to rid our world of unpleasant scenarios and painful feelings, trying to convince ourselves and/or others that we are somehow invincible! But the point here is that no matter what 'secret superhero powers' you believe you may have to complete your mission you will never succeed despite all your best efforts – all you will get is busier, more stressed and unhappier!

At this early stage, we wanted to share an acronym with you that might help you to remember what it is that we do to increase our busyness and stress and drain all the fun and fulfilment out of our lives, irrespective of how much we have to get down. This is: **BUSY**:

B **Believing and buying into our superhero mission.** How much time do you spend thinking through all the thoughts in your mind that tell you how busy you are, how much you have to get done, how you can't fail or let others or yourself down?

U **Unaware of our busy-causing habits and behaviours.** How often are you living life on autopilot, rushing around, remaining oblivious and unaware to what you are actually doing that really keeps you so busy?

S **Struggling with painful feelings, thoughts, sensations and behaviours.** How much time do you spend trying desperately hard to escape and avoid all discomfort and pain? Trying to get everything done and attended to, pleasing others and pursuing the obliteration of stress and discomfort in whatever you do?

Y **Yanking ourselves out of our present moment.** How much time do you spend in the present moment, or are you usually thinking about and looking to the past or the future or expecting the world to be different in some way, to find the answers to all your problems? Do you ever stop to savour the moment you are in (warts and all), or do you try ever so hard to rid your world of its imperfections, wishing and wanting another better time and place?

So how's about finally letting go of all this Busy Superhero facade? Is it really working for you? Can you imagine that amidst all the busyness and rushing around that you inevitably do, that you actually have the capacity to deal with life's imperfections and all of the stress and anxiety that arises in life? It may surprise you to know that you don't have to (nor can you) zap this stress into oblivion, eradicating all your pain once and for all, as if it were your superhero nemesis.

So, would you like to know how you can really feel less stressed, busy and pressured as you go about your challenging life? How about knowing how to stop this stress and pressure getting in the way of all the things that you want to get done and that are important to you, such as your work, your relationships with colleagues or loved ones or your physical health and well-being? Sound good? Or what about feeling at peace with a sense of satisfaction, even if you aren't able to complete your chores for the day? Can you imagine being able to calmly get through all the items on your to-do list with a greater sense of relaxation and grace? Would you like to bring more meaning and value to your life, rather than rushing around like a hysterical superhero? Well, now you truly can, and this book will show you just how to do all that. Through the transformative power of *Mindfulness* you will be able to find some peace and calm and a greater sense of well-being, productivity and life satisfaction irrespective of how uncomfortable, frantic and busy your life is.

> *"Through the transformative power of* Mindfulness *you will be able to find some peace and calm and a greater sense of well-being.*"

Here comes a final quick sell, we are going to show you how you can become immediately less stressed, less busy, more effective, efficient and focused, ready? Just a few minor adjustments ... shuffle about a bit, get comfy and see if you can *just* do this one exercise.

Exercise 2.2: Mindfulness reflection moment

Multitasking farce

As you read the paragraph below you must count all the times the letter 'e' appears. As you do this you must be counting and reading simultaneously – you can't read and then go back and count and you can't keep a record on a piece of paper – you have to do the counting in your head at the same time as reading the words on the page. In addition, accuracy is very important, so if you lose track or aren't 100% sure that you have counted correctly then you have to start all over again – that will happen at least once!

> Research consistently indicates that approximately 80% of the population experiences violent and upsetting thoughts. These thoughts are most likely due to automatic associations produced by the brain. In other words, there is no reflection on one's character for having a brain, which produces these thoughts. This idea is in stark contrast with a traditional therapeutic notion that the unconscious mind possesses deep-seated evil intentions. Given that intrusive thoughts are common, it would be unreasonable to strive for an absence of these thoughts.

Your answer (go on write it, we dare you, no one's looking!): _____

How did it go? Bit frustrating maybe? The answer is 52 by the way. Not so easy to focus on two (or more) things at once is it? So, to be less stressed, less busy and more effective, efficient and focused, forget the multitasking, because it is actually impossible to be truly effective at doing two things at once and will invariably stress you out. See how today, or for an hour, a few minutes even, you get along doing just one thing in the moment. Try it now as you read on, let go of any urges to count letters, check your mobile, tweet, drink coffee (we'll be doing that very soon in the next part of the book, we promise!), plan world domination or anything else that arises and see if you can allow yourself to *really* do just one thing at a time.

Mindfulness top tips to-go

In this chapter you have learned that it is helpful to:

- ▶ Recognise what Busy Superhero you may be trying to be.
- ▶ Notice that you may actually be creating more busyness for yourself.
- ▶ Recognise the fears that lurk behind all your busy behaviours.
- ▶ Try to stop doing everything at once, as multitasking just stresses you out even more and make you less effective.

CHAPTER

3

Understanding how to be mindful

In this chapter we are going to:

▶ Further develop our definition of what mindfulness is.

▶ Introduce you to an absolutely amazing part of your mind (well we think it is anyway).

▶ Help you understand how you can practise mindfulness using this.

▶ Start to practise some mindfulness.

The term mindfulness may seem a little mystical, psychological and unfamiliar or too abstract for many people, which is quite understandable. So, let's get straight to the point here, there is nothing alien about mindfulness; it is something that you have experienced numerous times in your life, probably as you go about most days, whatever age you are, whoever you are and whatever you get up to! You don't have to acquire it or get it in some way; it's with you already (and right here and now as you read this book), you've always had it and the ability to experience it, you just may want to understand it some more, reinforce and cultivate more of it (if only you had the time) and that is all this book is offering you, a way to do just that.

❝Mindfulness is a way of being rather than an object or thing that you attain.❞

Other terms that may feel a little more familiar or palatable that encapsulate and could be used interchangeably with the term mindfulness are: *awareness, consciousness, acknowledgement, observation* or *attention*. Mindfulness is a way of being rather than an object or thing that you attain and so it is even better understood and described by terms such as *noticing, knowing, observing, paying attention*, etc. It's your call, any will fit, it doesn't really matter anyway; we know what jam is, not because of the label on its jar but because of its taste, smell, texture and because of how it brings plain donuts, bland scones and dry toast to life! Mindfulness is all about showing up to your life, turning the lights up on the stage of your rich life experience to illuminate all that is going on for your observation and enjoyment – lap it all up, it's all yours for the taking (good and bad). It is all about bringing awareness and focusing your attention on your experience in a purposeful and particular way, with open curiosity and acceptance. Now does that sound better and clearer? If not, do read on …

❝Be fully present and connected to the experience that you are having in any given moment, in an accepting way.❞

As we said, the truth is that you are probably already familiar with the experience of mindfulness – to be fully present and connected to the experience that you are having in any given moment, in an accepting way. The outcome of all this is usually to feel stress-free, calm and still, to have clarity of mind and an overall sense of well-being. You have had this experience many times before (we are sure of that), all we are doing in this book is labelling this experience (mindfulness) and highlighting to you the process and recipe that brought it about for you so you can repeat it and do more of it when you want. Most people have described such an experience when doing vigorous exercise, playing an instrument or sitting in a serene setting, say on a beach watching the sunset. Others have described it while playing games and make-believe with their children (in fact, the way children demand our attention actually makes them excellent mindfulness teachers). In all these scenarios it may be that you have become fully immersed and engaged in your experience of the present moment, even losing track of time as you do so and somehow all your cares and worries seem far away. The truth is that the clock is still ticking away and any worries that you may have are still there in the background somewhere, but your current activity or surroundings have totally captivated your attention. Just think back to the happiest and/or most productive and meaningful moments of your life – we bet you were being mindful. The present moment really is a beautiful place to be and we are going to show you how you can spend more time there whenever you choose to.

Focus your attention, here and now!

Unlike in the common scenarios described above, we don't have to wait until we are suddenly drawn into being mindful because our life circumstances have changed (oh yes, I'll be mindful when the sunset attracts my attention). No, we can be mindful irrespective of the changing world around us or the ever-changing feelings that arise in us. It's all about YOU focusing your attention in a particular way (with acceptance) on your present moment experience, wherever you are, whatever you may be doing (the choice is yours in any given moment).

Mindfulness practices take many forms but essentially all of them share elements of cultivating a disciplined development of awareness – or you could say, the development of 'focused attention' on the present moment and seeing and experiencing that moment just how it is. Chogyam Trungpa, a Tibetan Buddhist monk and scholar, wrote of mindfulness:

> Mindfulness is like a microscope; it is neither an offensive nor defensive weapon in relation to the germs we observe through it. The function of the microscope is just to clearly present what is there. Mindfulness need not refer to the past or the future; it is fully now ... Awareness is seeing the discovery of mindfulness ... So mindfulness and awareness work together to bring acceptance of living situations as they are ... Life situations are the food of awareness and mindfulness; we cannot meditate without the depressions and excitements that go on in life.

The essence of mindfulness has been described by Teasdale (a mindfulness researcher) and his colleagues as a state of being:

> Fully present in the moment, without judging or evaluating it, without reflecting backwards on past memories, without looking forward to anticipate the future... and without attempting to 'problem-solve' or otherwise avoid any unpleasant aspects of the present situation.

It's time to wake up!

At the centre of mindfulness is acceptance, compassion and open curiosity towards yourself and the world around you (we will take a closer look at *compassion* and *curiosity* in some more detail, a little later); it's not about changing yourself but about accepting who you are and what you experience at any given moment. *But how can I do that? My thoughts are full of judgements and opinions about myself, others and the stuff around me!* Well you may be surprised to know that your thoughts are not the only part of your mind – you have another part of your mind called 'awareness', your *awareness mind,* and this part does not produce thoughts, opinions or judgements it just simply notices and acknowledges what is and how it is. It's the part of you that *knows* and is *aware* that you are thinking; IT IS YOU– stay with us now, here we go again (geeky stuff alert)...

Our brains have increased in size over the centuries from those of our primeval ancestors, and as you may know, we are now classified as Homo Sapien Sapien (we love our labels don't we, everything neatly and safely stored in cute, perfectly sized boxes, but what happens if something arises that doesn't fit into that box – well we often try desperately hard to knock it on the head, kill it off, delete and erase it IMMEDIATELY, oh, the struggles that we get ourselves into), which quite basically translates to: *Man (or woman) who is aware and is aware that s/he is aware.* Kind of amazing, huh? The sad thing is that we hardly ever use our awareness, we have the ability to be self-aware but we spend most of our time rushing around, gobbling down food, grabbing at what we want and running from what we don't like, acting on impulse, instinctively without much awareness at all, a bit like our cave-dwelling ancestors did (more about our ancient furry relatives to follow). Which often gets us into more trouble than it's all worth. So, in practice, do we ever actually use this amazing awareness part of our mind?

Awareness is central to mindfulness and being in this mode of your mind is how you cultivate more *acceptance* – in other words, mindfulness – as a way of being in life. We are going to discuss and understand more about our two different modes of our mind (thinking and awareness) in the next section of this book, but you have been patient enough, so let's start practising mindfulness right now.

Before you read on we ask that you take ten seconds now to try the following exercise, which will help you to notice the difference between your thinking mind (thoughts) and your 'awareness' mind. Yes, ten seconds (you read that right), that is all it takes!

Exercise 3.1: Mindfulness on-the-go

It only takes ten seconds

▷ When you have read through these simple instructions, close your eyes for the next ten seconds and try to notice and acknowledge the sensation in your body where your body makes contact with the surface on which you are sitting, laying or standing – this may be the sensation on your bottom or back where either meets the chair or bed, or the sensation on the soles of your feet where they meet the floor, if you are standing.

▷ Don't think about this sensation, just notice and acknowledge it, in other words hold it in your awareness, focus your attention on it and allow it to take centre stage at the forefront of your mind – nothing more than that.

▷ Should any thoughts pop into your mind about the exercise, any judgements or opinions about it or anything else at all (maybe about your body or what you need to get done generally), just notice these thoughts and bring your attention back to noticing and focusing on the sensation in your body.

▷ Just rest in awareness while you notice and concentrate on this sensation for ten seconds right now before reading on. Don't count the seconds just take a rough guess of how long to do the exercise for, during which try to pay full attention to the sensation in your body described above.

▷ As we said, it might help to close your eyes.

What did you notice? Did you notice the sensation in your body or thoughts in your mind or both? Most people report how they become more aware of their 'awareness' when doing this exercise and certainly about noticing the difference between being in 'awareness' versus being in their thinking mind. Don't worry if you weren't able to stay in your awareness mind for the whole ten seconds; that wasn't the goal anyway. It's more like a dance, our attention moving in and out of awareness, sometimes our thinking mind is taking the lead and at other times it's our awareness that leads. Just like a professional dancer or an athlete who both train to stay at the top of their game, we all need to train the mind to focus our attention and be more aware, and this takes practice.

> **“There are no thoughts in our 'awareness' therefore there is no cause of stress. ”**

It's also common for people to describe how they felt relaxed or a sense of stillness or peace when dropping into awareness. The reason for this is that there are no thoughts in our 'awareness' therefore there is no cause of stress. Being in awareness versus your thinking mind is to experience the most classic definition of the term *human being* (rather than *human-doing*); we are simply just *being*, being present to our experience right now, rather than *doing* anything about it. Despite all this, it is important to remember that dropping into awareness or truly noticing your experience in any given moment (in this instance a sensation in our body) is not a relaxation exercise (relaxation is just a fortunate by-product) but first and foremost an exercise of the mind. At first, it may feel a little strange to be in awareness, to be still, it feels weird for so many of us, as if there is something not right or weird about stillness, self-reflection or just *being* and *not doing*. If you felt odd, don't worry this is totally normal, we are so used to *doing* and rushing around it is understandable if this feels strange to begin with. If you didn't notice any of the above, put your book down and try the exercise again before you read any more.

With mindfulness, we can become aware and notice all manner of things and that's the beauty of everyday practice; we can just fit it into our busy lives without having to change anything, everything can just stay as it is, we can let it all be, while we focus our attention and rest in awareness of our experience.

Throughout this book and its practices, you will see that we encourage you to notice your breath here and there. We bet you wondered how long it would take us to mention that old hippy, tree-hugging cliché – ahh, and just breathe! But before you chuck this book down and ban it to the dark and dusty dungeon of yet-another-hippy-self-help-nonsense-read, listen – we are not talking about breath because we want you to try to relax or go all Zen on us (although that would be fine if you wanted to do either, of course) – the fact is that our breath is really a great way to reconnect to ourselves when everything around us is kicking up a storm. The beauty is that our breath is always with us, it's the only certainty that we have in life (apart from our death) as we go about our crazy busy existence. So, if you find you are not breathing, you have probably met with the other certainty and, if you are still breathing, good news … you can practise mindfulness with your breath whenever you like. It continues to go on, without any conscious effort from ourselves, always there, always present, our dear old reliable friend. Touching base with it by focusing our attention on it is often like a meta-phorical slap around our face (remember we said metaphorical – so no hitting PLEASE), a reality check when we are frantic, feeling stressed out and often off up, up and away with all our worrying thoughts. Dropping into awareness of our breath is stabilising and reassuring, we can use it to anchor ourselves to this present moment of reality (just as we can with the sensations in our body as we saw above) when it feels like the sh*t has, or is just about to, hit the fan!

> *Our breath is really a great way to reconnect to ourselves when everything around us is kicking up a storm.*

So here it is, let's get this over with nice and early, so we can move on to some other really great mindfulness exercises (that you may not have thought of). It's (usually) painless (but it might not be though – are you willing to give it a go anyway?) and like all the practices in this book its short, and you might even like it. You might want to use the audio guide to assist you with this practice (have a first read through the steps below before you begin).

Exercise 3.2: I haven't got time for this practice

The two-minute-breathing space

▶ So, close your eyes or rest your gaze on a still object or point in front of you.

▶ Drop into noticing your breath right now.

▶ You don't have to change your breathing or alter it in any way, no need to push or pull on your breath.

▶ Just notice it, as it naturally is, its natural rhythm and sensations.

▶ See if you can notice the sensation of cool air rise into your nostrils as you breathe in and the warmer sensation of breath leaving your nostrils as you breathe out.

▶ Pay attention to the rise of your stomach as you breathe in and the falling of your stomach as you breathe out.

▶ There it is – your breath, with its natural rhythm and sensations, in this moment.

▶ And then there's you noticing your breath in this moment.

▶ Remain aware of your breath, ride the waves of your breathing with your full attention.

▶ Follow each in breath from its beginning to its natural end.

▶ Follow each out breath from its beginning to its natural end.

▶ See if you can notice and acknowledge the pause at the end of each in breath before it loops to turn into the next out breath.

▶ See if you can notice the pause at the end of each out breath before it loops back to turn into the next new in breath.

▶ Allow your breath to take centre stage in your awareness right now.

▶ No matter how many times your attention may wander from your breath (remember this is normal and what human minds do), you may be distracted by thoughts, sounds, feelings or sensations, just notice the distraction and gently guide your attention back to noticing your breathing.

▶ Just this breath, just this moment, right here and right now.

▶ Allow your breathing, as it is, with its sensations and rhythm to take centre stage in your awareness.

▶ After a few more mindful breaths, open your eyes and notice and acknowledge a few objects around you, see if you can continue to drop into awareness using your breath as a focal point, as you continue your day.

So how was that? Not so bad we assume, if it was then what did you notice, what was difficult? Was it annoying, frustrating, was it difficult to focus your attention? What expectations or thoughts were getting in the way? Did you try too hard to get it right? Mindfulness is a discipline; it's simple but not always so easy. The mind is so unruly and highly conditioned that it's hard to stay focused. But mindfulness also has a great way of highlighting all this, our habitual tendencies and struggles. Hold onto that point for now, we are going to come back to it soon enough.

When you are feeling stressed, busier than you could possibly ever be, we encourage you to come back to noticing your breathing in this way – it doesn't have to take long at all, a minute or so (or less) will do, wherever you are, whatever you are doing. You may find that there is no stress or busyness in that very moment, just clarity, resting in awareness of your breath.

There are loads of further mindfulness exercises to come, that will not only start to help you develop greater awareness, acceptance, curiosity and compassion but will also help you to begin to experience some every-day activities and objects in a whole new light. In the next part of this book, we are going to look more closely at how mindfulness can help you to manage your busy, stressful life. There are lots more insights and practices to follow – we have only just begun!

Mindfulness top tips to go

In this chapter you have learned that it is helpful to:

▶ See mindfulness as something that you already have and are familiar with.

▶ Understand mindfulness as cultivating a part of our mind called 'awareness'.

▶ Recognise that awareness is key to being mindful.

▶ Understand that practising 'being aware' is crucial to mindfulness.

▶ Become aware of your breathing as a practice and to help you reconnect and make contact with the present moment when you feel stress.

Part 1 summary

In this first part of the book, you have:

▶ Gained an understanding of mindfulness and how it might be useful for many aspects of your life.

▶ Begun to learn what it is that makes you busy in life.

▶ Understood how mindfulness can benefit you amidst your busy life.

▶ Understood how you can become more mindful.

▶ Begun to practise mindfulness through 'awareness'.

▶ Started to practise mindfulness and noticed what it is like being in this mode of your mind.

Check out the next part of this book, if you are now keen to:

▶ Further your insights and practice of mindfulness;

▶ Get a firmer hold on and an understanding of your busy life; and

▶ Develop and practice some specific acceptance techniques and mindfulness exercises that will really help you to manage some of the stress that you might experience throughout your busy days.

Keep reading, we have some very special treats in store for you.

Part

2

Mindfulness and our mental lives

Our crazy world is just in our head

Now that we have introduced the basic principles of mindfulness and highlighted the ways in which it can help you with your busy life, and demonstrated how to start to practise it, we are now keen to turn your attention to *busyness* and *stress* because, let's face it, busyness wouldn't be a problem at all if it felt nice and wasn't stressful, now would it? So in this second part of the book we will illustrate to you in some more detail how mindfulness can help with the inevitable stress that you will experience as you go about your busy life. We are specifically going to turn your attention to:

▷ What exactly it is that creates more busyness and stress for us.

▷ How we can create more time without changing a thing around us or any of our life circumstances.

▷ Why and how we became such busy creatures.

▷ What happens when we start to feel really stressed and what we can do to feel less stressed.

▷ Look at the busy world that goes on in our mind: our thoughts.

▷ Practise lots of mindfulness.

The 'perfect illusion' – chasing a stress-free existence

In the first chapter of this second part of the book, we're going to:

▶ Reveal the *real* cause and exacerbating factors of your busyness and stress.

▶ Show you how you can start to become less stressed and less busy with just a few simple insights and techniques.

▶ Help you understand how your *relationship* with your busyness is actually the real problem to address rather than expecting the world around you to change.

Sorry to break it to you so suddenly like this, but if you're hoping to find something that will suddenly make you become purely and constantly stress-free – maybe once you've got all your chores done or got that perfect job, cash in the bank, given face time to Facebook to like all your LinkedIn link-ups, or even after reading this book – then we're afraid to say that you're most certainly barking up the wrong tree! We're certainly not offering you a quick-fix to all your stress and busyness and a one-way ticket along easy street towards everlasting happiness. Mindfulness is not a short cut to this at all, but any time that you can invest in practising it, it will be worthwhile (we promise – and you know us by now, we are not in the 'game' to serve up false promises).

Now, as you read this you're probably thinking *well yes, of course I know that, I'm never going to suddenly always be stress-free, totally calm and happy*, but if you're being really honest with yourself consider how much time you spend analysing your life, trying to think through all that is going wrong, problem-solving, daydreaming about how you would like things to be, planning and plotting your next move to bring about your everlasting happiness and peace. How many of your fantasies and thoughts in life are secretly based on and motivated by this illusionary belief? How many times have you thought that if only things were different, if only you could get all this stuff sorted out, done and dusted, then you would be happy, forever? Be honest with yourself now!

Now with this in mind, consider how many of your worries and resulting pursuits, actions and day-to-day tasks are motivated by this belief – how much time do you spend busily rushing around in an attempt to get everything done so you can finally eradicate all the stress and busyness in your life and feel happy and relaxed once and for all?

If you are striving for this fantasy we can assure you that you will find yourself rushing around like a hamster on a wheel indefinitely. Without addressing this preoccupation lurking within our thoughts and behind our actions, we run the risk of exhaustion, burnout, increasing levels of stress and even more busyness. We are also more prone to a whole host of more debilitating psychological and other health-related problems to boot – not to mention decreasing levels of well-being, productivity, creativity, vitality and generally less satisfaction and fulfilment in life. As we rush around pursuing this illusion, on autopilot, unaware of it and all the thoughts, fantasies, feelings and behaviours that fuel it, we are actually missing out on much of our lives. Most of us busy people seem preoccupied with another 'perfect', blissfully peaceful time and place and spend much of our energy rushing around chasing our tails to find it, indefinitely! This preoccupation makes us inefficient, it holds us back in life and it is time-consuming. It is, however, very much alive and laying just beneath our busy experience for most of us busy people, it's constantly pulling us out of the very moment that we are living in now, in anticipation of a fantasy (that will never come) and all we get as a result of pursuing this fantasy is an even greater sense of busyness and fewer fulfilments in life.

> *Busy people seem preoccupied with another 'perfect', blissfully peaceful time and place and spend much of their energy rushing around to find it.*

Exercise 4.1: Mindfulness reflection moment

How connected to your life are you, really?

Consider whether you have experienced any of the following scenarios over the past week as you have been either daydreaming about how your life should be less hectic and/or planning and plotting your next tactical manoeuvre as you work your way through your never-ending to-do lists:

- Zoned out of conversations and forgotten what others have said to you.
- Arrived at destinations without any idea of how you got there.
- Gobbled down breakfast/lunch/dinner 'on the go' without ever actually tasting your food.
- Paid more attention to your iPhone or tablet than to your colleagues, friends or family.
- Dwelt on the past or worried about the future.
- Skim-read pages of this book!

If you have experienced any or all of these scenarios, then it's likely that you have been living on autopilot, been too caught up inside your thoughts and fantasies of how you think your life should be and caused yourself more stress, more busyness and generally taken less satisfaction from your life. These kinds of behaviours represent clues that may remind you how you often choose to mindlessly create more busyness and less satisfaction in your life. It is worth taking a few moments to extend the exercise above to ask yourself the following questions:

Exercise 4.2: Mindfulness reflection moment

Am I my own worst enemy?

How do you disconnect from your life experience?

▶ Are you constantly caught up in the thoughts whizzing around your mind?

▶ Do you notice the world around you as you rush about your life?

▶ Do you ever stop for a moment for no other reason but to notice how you feel emotionally or physically, or what you might need – such as food, water, care, attention?

How do you avoid and try to get rid of stress and busyness in your life?

▶ Do you try to do more and more in the hope that soon enough everything will be done and dusted and you can kick back, relax and rest?

▶ Do you drink more alcohol, smoke cigarettes or take drugs to feel less stressed, to get out of your head and get rid of painful, stressful feelings?

▶ Do you veg out in front of the TV or withdraw from loved ones to avoid more hassle and stress in your life?

Are you fearful of failing or being judged by others?

▶ Does this lead you to try to be perfect in everything you do? Do you constantly say 'yes' or immediately respond to all and sundry that asks of you?

Are you preoccupied with worry and stressful thoughts?

▶ Does your mind race with stressful thoughts about what you should be doing, what you haven't done, maybe how you are not good enough and you should be doing more and better?

Are you engaged with your busy story?

▶ Constantly replaying this script, telling yourself and anyone else who can bear to listen how busy you are, how much you have to get done, how unfair and stressful your life is?

Do you ever stop to really consider what is most important to you in life?

▶ How does 'doing' busy affect your mental and physical health, well-being, vitality, relationships?

▶ How would you liked to be remembered when your time is up, how would you like to know that you lived your life – as a busy and stressed person or a caring, connected, efficient, calm, compassionate person, maybe?

Lap it up!

We are so preoccupied with all that we have to get done that even if we do find we have five minutes to kill here and there, we usually use that time to think through what we should be doing or where we should be next or replaying some past encounter or mishap over and over in our mind or worry about what is coming up. We miss out on so much of our experience this way. What about coffee breaks? How often have you really enjoyed a 'break' when you've had your 'coffee/cigarette/tea (or whatever you do) break'?

These mini intervals throughout the day are rarely that, or moments of any form of rest or coffee satisfaction, in fact they are often just another habit, full of other mini habits being lived out on autopilot (without much awareness) at the same time. Often when we sit to have a brief coffee break, whether that be throughout the day, or in the morning before we leave for work, or any other time, we become instantly caught up in all the habitual thinking patterns in our mind, like what we have or often haven't managed to tick off the to-do list beforehand and what we will endeavour to get done and complete once we have finished our coffee/break. If it's not this then we may find ourselves in some fantasy land, daydreaming for a short while about somewhere else or another time. We are also often doing more things at the same time, such as getting dressed, reading some paperwork, talking to someone, watching TV or listening to the radio. How many times do you really just sit and have a cup of coffee, for no other reason at all than just that?

> *"How many times do you really just sit and have a cup of coffee, for no other reason at all than just that?"*

The purpose of the next exercise is to begin to show you just how you can bring and incorporate mindfulness into your everyday activities (we will be doing much more of this throughout the remainder of the book), such as drinking coffee. It will show you how you have the power to break old habits and live a more meaningful and enjoyable life. Sure, it's only coffee/tea/a cigarette (or whatever it may be), you might say – but the awareness you bring to this experience is the key to a more meaningful life. Remember, this is not about coffee but about *pure awareness* and therefore *acceptance*. This exercise will allow you to start to use your coffee interludes for the reason they were intended – to have a break from the endless rushing around that you do all day long – often inside your head. If you don't like or drink coffee you can try this exercise with any other drink you choose (or even a cigarette if you smoke – just be aware and curious in the same way as outlined below). If you drink your coffee in public, don't worry about anyone noticing what you are doing, as you drink it mindfully, they'll just think that you are deep in thought – which is what most of them will be doing anyway and secretly what you're not doing! Here are some further pointers before you give it a go:

- ▶ Should any thought pop into your mind, about what you are doing, any judgement or opinion about the exercise, preferences about the taste of the coffee, what others may be thinking if they can see you, or anything else at all, just notice that these thoughts are there and bring your attention back to noticing your experience of drinking the coffee as outlined below.

- ▶ Remember, there is no agenda to have any particular experience of drinking your coffee – the only goal is to pay attention to whatever your experience is.

- ▶ So go get a cup of coffee (or whatever your vice may be) and try this practice out now or as soon as you can.

- ▶ You might like to use the audio guide to assist you in this practice.

Exercise 4.3: I haven't got time for this practice

Wake up and smell the coffee

▶ First, hold your cup of coffee in both hands (and if you usually do this, experiment by holding it some other way). Notice the weight of the coffee cup plus the liquid inside it. Notice the heat of the cup against your hands and fingers.

▶ Acknowledge the fact and be aware that you are noticing the weight and the heat of the cup. There's the weight and the heat of the coffee cup and then there's you noticing it. Allow the weight and heat of the coffee cup to take centre stage in your awareness.

▶ Don't worry if you can't feel the weight or heat enough or properly, remember this is not about the weight and heat, it's about awareness and acceptance of what is.

▶ Bring the coffee cup closer to your face and notice the aroma, soaking it up as it fills the space in front of your face.

▶ It is natural for your attention to wander or become distracted, when this happens just gently guide it back to noticing your coffee and the sensations you experience.

▶ Now, as you bring the cup closer to your mouth in anticipation of the first sip, notice the movement in your body, hands and of your lips.

▶ Acknowledge the fact and be aware that you are noticing the movement in your body, hands and lips. There's the movement in your body, hands and lips and then there's you noticing this movement. Allow the movement in your body, hands and lips to take centre stage in your awareness.

▶ Now, as you take a sip of coffee, notice the temperature of the warm liquid enter your mouth and any physical responses in your body.

▶ Notice and experience the taste of the coffee.

▶ Be aware that you are noticing the taste of the coffee.

▶ Before you swallow, notice the natural impulse to swallow. Once you have swallowed, notice how your body is one sip of coffee heavier.

▶ Now, notice the gap of time after you have swallowed before you take the next sip of coffee into your mouth.

▶ Your experiences of drinking coffee change – but the part of you that notices these experiences does not change, it remains pure and simply aware, nothing more, nothing less.

▶ Should your attention wander or become distracted, just gently guide it back to noticing your coffee and any sensation that you experience.

There's no more time to waste!

Sure enough, with all that is going on in your life right now, with all the stuff that you have to get done, all the places that you have to be, all that you have to attend to and tick off your never-ending to-do list, there must be as many frustrating obstacles, barriers and annoying people and situations that get in your way every day – we know that we're often *f'ing and blinding* our way through most days, full of indignation and resentment, *if only those stupid people would get a move on I could catch my train on time!* Sound familiar? Like us, if you're feeling busy and stressed, you probably spend most of your time rushing from one task to the next pointing the finger in blame at anyone or anything that slows you down – they are the reason that you are stressed and busier than you should be! Woe betide the next person that gets in our way!

The truth is that there is nothing else to blame for our busyness, no one else, no endless emails, no after-school activities, no relentless work projects, no annoying friends, uncaring partners, demanding bosses or slack colleagues – in fact nothing else at all is responsible for our escalating stress levels, frantic rushing, gruesome schedules and general busyness, except ourselves! It is our fantasies and thoughts about how unfair our busy lives are and our endless pursuit to eradicate all our busyness (and the associated discomfort and painful feelings that go with it) and to finally find and secure a place of peace, calm and everlasting happiness that really keeps us busy and stressed out. Try making a list or having a think right now of all the things that you assume make you more stressed and busier in life. We've listed a few of our own recurring rants to help you get started:

Exercise 4.4: Mindfulness reflection moment

What slows you down and makes you stressed and busier?

1 Waiting in queues.
2 Moving through a crowd on the tube.
3 Traffic jams/roadwork delays.
4 Losing your phone/no internet connection.
5 Others taking ages to make their point.
6 **ME, MYSELF and I!**

What if the next time you are in a situation such as the ones listed above (or any others that you came up with), that instead of becoming sucked into a rant about how everything is in your way, how delayed and slowed down you are, what you have to do next, focusing on the outcome and how you won't be able to get everything done, fantasising how your life should be versus how you are experiencing it in that moment and generally being caught up in all the frustration that arises with this, that you actually just become aware of this fantasy-fuelled rant that is a result of frustration and anxiety, nothing more and nothing less than that. Just notice who or what exactly is making you more stressed out and increasing your sense of busyness in that very moment – is it the situation and people around you, the buzz of the endless message alerts going off on your phone or YOU and all the worrying and frustration that you are *doing* about the situation? From a moment of awareness such as this you will no doubt notice that no other person or thing is exacerbating your stress and busyness – that's just you!

Time is ticking away!

As we rush around amidst our busyness it all too often seems as if there simply isn't enough time in the day to get everything done– tick, tock, tick, tock – ARGH! However, time simply ticks away at the same pace for everyone, every day, whether it feels like it is going faster or not. The reason that on some days it seems to whizz past us faster than the speed of light is often all down to our worry about it slipping away, our worry that there just never is enough time in the day. While we are worrying in this way, we are simply not present or 'awake' enough to actually experience real time at all – that's right we are living in the land of the fairies (usually mean ones) once again, our fantasy land of worry and anticipation: all that we have to do, all the time that it will take, all the time that we don't have, etc.

The truth is that most of us are continuously yanking ourselves (hopefully metaphorically) out of the very present moment of reality by worrying in anticipation of that very moment passing by – that's why there never seems to be any time left to get all and sundry taken care of. Most of us are just not very good at using real time in a helpful way at all. We tend to waste time away by worrying about it passing most of the time. Take Sandra in the following case example for instance, she worried that she had no time for herself (and it's fair to say like the rest of us, she had a lot on and to take care of) but in all her worry about this she missed the point that she actually had loads of time for herself – the same amount of time that we all have.

Sandra

When Sandra came to therapy she was in tears and she looked exhausted. She was busy, busy, busy – dividing her time between her husband, her three children, her work and her friends. She explained that she was working hard to not leave anyone out and she carefully planned her days so that she gave everyone and everything the time that she felt they deserved – the sad fact was that she never felt that she had any time left for herself. She fantasised about taking long hot baths, to get her hair done, to do some shopping, to curl up on the sofa with her book. But the more she fantasised about all this, it just upset her more and the more she felt increasingly busier and as if there wasn't ever enough time in the day for her. The reality was that Sandra was just too preoccupied with time and how she didn't have enough of it – sure her life was busy and demanding but even in the face of this fact she had ample time for herself and she just didn't see it, she spent most of it worrying that she never had it! Her time was not restricted in any way at all, it was in fact abundant just as it is for all of us, no matter how busy we are. Sandra was waiting for a time when there weren't any demands on her, to take time for herself, the truth is that in every moment – whether she was spending time with others or not – she always had the possibility to spend time with herself also.

All time is *my time*!

> *"Everywhere you are, everywhere you go, whatever you are doing and whomever you are with – surprise, surprise, you are also there!"*

When our life is so busy we feel the need to allocate time to tasks, which can of course be helpful, but we must try to remember that all this time is in fact *our* time. You can learn to bring awareness to your everyday experiences with mindfulness (there's loads more ideas to come a bit later of how you can practise mindfulness on the go) and inasmuch feel that you have ample and unlimited time to spend with yourself. Everywhere you are, everywhere you go, whatever you are doing and whomever you are with – surprise, surprise, you are also there! So as you go about your everyday busy routine make a conscious effort to check in with your experience of that moment – you might run through a quick list of short questions as outlined in the exercise below, to silently answer to yourself that will help you to feel present, taken care of (by yourself!) and attended to.

Exercise 4.5: Mindfulness on-the-go

Spending time with yourself wherever you are

1 How am I feeling right now?
2 How am I standing, walking, sitting right now?
3 How does my body feel right now?
4 What am I doing right now?
5 What thoughts am I thinking right now?
6 What do I *really* need in this moment?
7 What is really important to me right now?
8 How would I like to be in this moment?
9 What do I want to stand for in the face of this situation I am in?
10 Is buying into these thoughts or acting in this way helping me live a productive and meaningful life?
11 How connected to my present life experience am I right now?

Letting time slip away

You may be thinking that you can't let go of time, planning and working to timed schedules – surely that would be insane! How on earth will you get deadlines met, everything done, organised, executed and delivered if all you do is all this 'airy, fairy' mindfulness stuff? Well we are not advising that you let go of time altogether, to be time-sensitive is helpful to navigate yourself throughout your busy life and any of the projects and tasks that you want to get done every day. But there is a large discrepancy between, on the one hand, considering and planning your routine around time, allocating time to specific activities and, on the other, spending all your time worrying that there isn't enough time and never actually feeling alive, present in the moment and that you are able to enjoy any given moment of your time as a consequence.

Keeping a track of time does not interfere with being present in any given moment or the practice of mindfulness whatsoever, please do be assured of that. That said, time itself and our relationship to it are entirely part of our constructions of the world, they are not 'real' any more than days of the week, months or years are 'real'. Time is simply a useful construct to help orient ourselves and coordinate ourselves with others. Just like any event in the world we can make various meanings from this and judge ourselves and others in relation to these. Being 'punctual', 'rushing', 'late', 'slovenly' or 'lazy' usually all entail some concept of time, as do many other ideas of our identity such as our time in history, age and sense of achievement or milestones. Sometimes it is helpful to reflect on how time serves us in these ways, or whether it can feed into habitual patterns of our *thinking* mind (more of this to come) that take us away from the present and away from the moment we are in, this can give us an overwhelming sense of time slipping away further adding to a sense of always trying to play catch-up. However, if you bring more present focused awareness to your experience at any given moment (as outlined in the **Mindfulness on-the-go** exercise above), you will find that time doesn't seem to slip away so often.

One of the best ways to develop a more helpful relationship with time is to practise mindfulness of a watch or clock. A dial watch, rather than a digital watch is much easier to start to practise with. A dial watch gives us a spatial representation of time – we just *know* what time it is by looking at the face of the watch or clock and noticing and acknowledging what time it is without *thinking* about or trying to work out the time too much – knowing what time it is doesn't have to stimulate any thoughts, it doesn't actually require any further thinking or calculations or further planning whatsoever. We don't have to think about it or work the time out or how much more time we may have left to do what we are doing – usually we visualise and know all this by observing where the hands of the clock are – we just simply *know* the time. By contrast, when we read the time from a digital display we often start to think about and calculate the time and how much time we have left to do something or get somewhere etc. You might even notice that there is a lot more to be mindful and aware of with a dial watch particularly if it ticks, and/or has a date display. Just notice and know the time, date and sounds that your watch is displaying, nothing more and nothing less, as often as you can over the next week. If you tend to check the time on your smartphone, set the time display to a dial (maybe download an app for this) and give that a go over the next week also.

Try the following mindfulness exercise with a dial display of time as outlined below as often as you like. Use it to help you cultivate a different relationship with time, to let go of all the pressure that you often associate with time ticking away. You can allocate as much time as you want to do this practice, and you can see when to stop as you will be checking and observing (but not thinking about!) the time throughout. You might like to use the audio recording to assist you with this practice.

Exercise 4.6: I haven't got time for this practice

Watching time – tick, tock!

1 Look at a watch or clock and check the time now. Know, acknowledge and notice but don't think about, what time it is.

2 Be aware that you are noticing the time. There is no need to think about or calculate what time it is at all, see it, know it, there it is, the time.

3 Acknowledge where the hour hand, minute hand and second hand are.

4 Notice the difference in space between these hands.

5 Notice the sound if any, that is coming from the watch or clock.

6 Notice the silence in between the sounds it makes.

7 Should any thoughts about what you are doing, the time in general, what time it is or isn't, how much time you have left, what a waste of time this is, or any others show up at all, just notice these thoughts,

let go of them, congratulate yourself for noticing them, and let them drift by as you bring your attention back to noticing, acknowledging and knowing the time right now, in this moment.

8 There it is, the time, and then there's you noticing the time.

9 Should any feelings show up, any anxiety, boredom or frustration, just acknowledge these feelings, congratulate yourself for acknowledging them, and gently guide your attention back to observing time and knowing the time right now.

10 There it is, the time, and then there is you noticing and knowing the time.

11 Your experiences of watching the time change, your thoughts, feelings about the time come and go, but the you that simply knows, notices and is aware of the time does not change.

12 There's time and then there's you noticing and knowing the time

It all began with a 'busy' caveman

As we rush around frantically and tirelessly pursuing everlasting happiness (and we have so many more ways that this illusion is now presented as possible to us – just watch the segment leading into the advert break of a TV show such as Britain's Got Talent or The X-Factor, to remind yourself of what we mean by this – oh, the false promises of a blissful life and it all sounds so easy to win), we are actually using the same part of our brain as our cave-dwelling ancestors used when they strove for survival amidst an unfamiliar and threatening world – our flight or fight response.

Sure, unlike cavemen we may not be running from wild animals today, but we are 'running' towards perfection, success, happiness and relaxation, and simultaneously we are 'running away' from the opposite (imperfection, failure, unhappiness, *busyness*) – a threat, just the same as wild animals were to our cavemen ancestors.

Today striving for complete perfection, relaxation and happiness via our endless attempts at thinking through and analysing our life problems, evaluating our lives and how we would prefer them to be and then acting on the back of all these thoughts (such as phoning in to answer the simple competition question to try and win a prize that will take all our woes away, or trying to desperately tick off the never ending to-do list, securing our place in the millionaire's club, or that perfect relationship, family, home, job, body, etc.), the more our bodies release the same amount of cortisol and adrenalin, our stress hormones, and the more we

come to experience the same level of anxiety and stress throughout much of our daily lives as our ancestors did running from wild animals centuries ago. The less busy we try to become the busier we are!

"The less busy we try to become the busier we are!"

In their necessary survival mode, our cave-dwelling ancestors evolved to develop a strong sense of fear to keep them on high alert for the next potential danger. They felt uneasy most of the time as a result, as they constantly scanned their environment for threats. Our brains today have not evolved much over the centuries and in this respect we continue to be on high alert to the next potential looming problem or danger that may bring about our very own modern-day downfalls. Of course there are less physical threats to our survival these days, but nonetheless we do still inherently scan our present-day, busy lives for potential threats to our survival – and let's face it there's a lot of stuff that poses a threat these days! As we mentioned earlier, there's work to get done, there's jobs to keep, bills to pay, kids to get to school and feed, homework and housework to be done, emails to answer, friends and family to keep happy, health and fitness to maintain etc., to name just a few of the standard tasks that most of us feel the need to get done and sorted daily. This plethora of activity and tasks can leave us feeling highly stressed, exhausted and not to mention defeated when everything is not ticked off the to-do list at the end of each day.

Our preoccupation with these threats is learned and motivated by our attempts to eradicate any feelings of failure and rejection in life – or in other words, to avoid our modern-day downfall and ensure our survival, just as our ancestors did many years ago. We have learned from our ancient, scatty predecessors that the feelings of failure and rejection are connected to our decline, our ceasing to survive – they are scary and must be avoided at all costs (more of this to come in the next part of this book) so we try anything and everything to eradicate (which isn't possible) or hide or escape these scary feelings as much as we can.

The learned survival 'gift' from our ancestors is never asleep and constantly ticking away in our thoughts in the form of our worrying, reminiscing, problem-solving, analysing, planning and evaluating. It is constantly alert to all that we don't have, all that we haven't done, all that might go horribly wrong, all that we can't cope with due to the way that we feel, and others' negative appraisals of us. If we remain unaware of it while it is on autopilot then we run the risk of it going into overdrive, leading to more stress and physical aches and pains, more inefficiency, and all the life discomfort and dissatisfaction that we will inevitably come to experience as a result.

So how do I switch off this survival mechanism? Quick, I need to know! I have so much more to get on with and I can't let it get in the way! We hear you exclaim. Well, there it goes again, we'd say, in the form of your worrying (caveman/woman) thoughts. Noticing it is the key, as becoming aware of it is much the same as overriding it, because you simply can't do it (worry) and be aware of it (notice your worry) at the same time. We are going to explain exactly what we mean by this and show you how to develop this ability of awareness further and specifically around our stressful thoughts later in this part of the book (Chapter 6), but here's just a bit more to get you *noticing* and thinking about first.

Down the stress well

Our experience of stress comes in all shapes and sizes. We experience racing thoughts, painful emotions, uncomfortable bodily sensations and we also find ourselves doing lots of busy behaviours. These experiences are just that, experiences that come and go. What usually happens is that we over-identify with them as if they are us. We might hear ourselves saying stuff like; 'I am stressed' or 'I am exhausted' – well the truth is that you are neither, you are YOU and you are experiencing stressful feelings in your emotions, and sensations of tiredness in your body in that moment – there's a big difference. With mindful awareness we can stand back from our experiences such as thoughts, feelings, physical sensations and behaviours and see them for what they are, fleeting experiences that come and go naturally. When we don't do this and instead get caught up in them, trying to eradicate them, we simply exacerbate our distress. Take Clare for example, the more she over-identified and got caught up with her experiences of stress the more she escalated them.

> ❝We can stand back from our experiences such as thoughts, feelings, physical sensations and behaviours and see them for what they are, fleeting experiences.❞

Claire

There's no denying the fact that Clare had a busy life. She was the mother of three children, two daughters and one son, aged seven, six and two years old respectively. She worked part-time in human resources of a large corporate bank and also did some charity work on the weekends with bereaved children. She was a housewife the rest of the time and also helped care for her elderly mother who had been suffering with worsening Alzheimer's over the last year. Her eldest children were at school and doing quite well and her son spent most of the time with her throughout the day. It's not surprising that Clare had a few to-do lists on the go at the same time, which she hardly ever felt that she was able to get on top of.

One Thursday morning after she dropped her daughters off at school, Clare returned home to have a much needed cup of coffee while she checked her work emails before she intended to begin some of the housework. Her son was a little under the weather with a cough and she wanted to take him to the GP to make sure that everything was OK. As she opened her email account an email popped up marked as urgent. With some trepidation, Clare opened the email, which was from her manager at work asking her to help out that weekend with finalising a presentation that had to be delivered to a client the following week. Her heart sank; there was no way that she could fit that in on top of all the other tasks she had to get through between now and Sunday.

Clare's thoughts began to race through her mind and she started to get caught up in the content of her thoughts: how am I supposed to do this on top of everything else? I simply can't do it, but I can't let them down, they're relying on me and will probably think I can't handle the job if I say no to this! Maybe I can do it, but then again I just can't! As she thought this way and got more caught up in her stressful thoughts, trying to work her

➤

problem out, she became more and more emotionally anxious, she then began to notice her heart racing in her body and her hands trembling. She felt dizzy, she thought she might be having a heart attack or that her body was failing her generally, so she decided to go and lay down on her bed for a second. As she lay there, she realised that she had left her son playing alone in the TV room. She began to think about what a bad mother she was for taking this action, and how if she laid around all day like this she was never going to get him to the GP like she had planned. Clare began to feel even more anxious.

As we can see from Clare's example, she experienced stress in four different ways or parts of her internal experience: in her thoughts (I can't do this), her emotions (anxiety), her bodily sensations (racing heart and trembling hands) and her behaviour (lying on the bed). Instead of allowing these experiences to come and go, she got too caught up with them, and assumed they were either fixed states, representations of her or that she had to try to get rid of them and she judged herself for having them. All this just seemed to lead to higher levels of stress and anxiety.

This habitual reaction to our experiences of stress is common to all of us at times of distress. If we remain unaware of it happening, it will continue to live itself out on autopilot, increasing our overall stress levels until we eventually become completely burnt-out, or more depressed and/or anxious. We need to stand back from these experiences (in the form of our thoughts, emotions, sensations and behaviours) and notice them for what they are – THEY ARE NOT US, but simply passing experiences for us that we can observe and let go of. Mindfulness is exactly how we do just that.

The never-ending to-do lists: how they affect our busyness and our confidence

Like Clare, many of us busy people have one if not many more ongoing to-do lists that we feel help us to navigate through our busy lives. We may have one for work and at least one other for home or personal tasks that we have to attend to. These lists are often broken down into maintenance-type tasks for the sort of things that are essential to keep things ticking over and also tasks regarding new ventures or projects that are there with good intention to further our working or personal lives. Here's another to-do list for you to consider – have a go at thinking through the following exercise.

Exercise 4.7: Mindfulness reflection moment

To do or not to do

Prioritise this list (1 being the most important, 10 being the least):

- Write a 'to-do-list'.
- Add more jobs to list.
- Lose list.
- Try to remember all jobs to do.
- Find old list.
- Amalgamate to-do lists.
- Tick off jobs done.
- Underline jobs not done.
- Create some more jobs.
- Make a new list.

The truth is that the more and more we add to our to-do lists the more overwhelming they become and the more we feel unable to tackle them and get the items ticked off. It is often the case that we take a momentary glance at our list only to find ourselves then brushing it aside to get on with some other tasks that may bring some more instant positive emotional reward instead, such as booking a holiday online or generally surfing the web. Why is this then, when surely we have learned from our past experience that we can complete and tick off tasks from our lists? Is it not the case, that despite our to-do lists feeling overwhelming or unappealing at the very least, we still at times manage to get items ticked off and come to realise afterwards with hindsight that cleaning out the kitchen cupboards or filing our tax return wasn't really that bad after all and we even reap some great sense of reward and achievement in completing such a task?

Well, when we get caught up with the thoughts in our mind, such as *I can't do it*, they not only affect our mood, physical sensations and behaviour as we saw in Clare's example above but paying attention to such thoughts in this way (listening to their content), also has a detrimental impact on our level of self-confidence underneath all this stress and busyness on the surface. This is an affect that we might not immediately recognise, but if we just take a look at our tendency to put off tackling items on our to-do lists, this effect on our confidence becomes really quite apparent.

The more we glance at our to-do lists and listen to the content of thoughts such as *I can't do it, it's too difficult, I haven't got the energy, it will be boring, I'm not in the mood*, etc., the more we are commenting on our *failings* and therefore the more we undermine our self-confidence. This then leads to procrastination and putting things off in our behaviour (and an ever-increasing to-do list and resulting sense of busyness to boot!) as we don't feel that we have the capacity or confidence to tolerate the boredom and emotional strain that doing some mundane task, such as completing our tax return, will bring to us. So, even though we may have learned that we can complete tasks and reap the positive rewards in doing so, remaining engaged in such self-critical thoughts, such as *I can't do this*, continues to undermine our self-confidence nonetheless.

Mindfulness top tips to-go

In this chapter you have learned how it is helpful to:

▶ Watch your tendency to try to secure everlasting happiness and a blissfully stress-free time (it will only make you busier and more stressed).

▶ Notice how all your attempts at being less busy actually dampen down your rich life experience.

▶ Try to worry less that there is no time for you as this will only create the illusion of there being less time.

▶ Watch your habitual tendency to over-identify, struggle and get caught up in judgement, with your experiences of stress (in the form of thoughts, feeling, sensations and behaviours).

▶ Try not to buy into unhelpful thoughts (we are going to show you exactly how you can do this in Chapter 6) as they will negatively affect your mood, self-confidence and general stress experience.

5

To be or not to be busy?

In this chapter you will learn:

- ▶ More about how it is that we actually keep our own sense of busyness alive.

- ▶ What busy story you have, that makes you feel even busier in life.

I have too much to do
There's no way that I can get all this done in time
It's not fair!
My life is overwhelming
Why can't others do more or just get out of my bl***y way!

Do any of these statements sound familiar? If so, it's likely that you are feeling pretty busy and stressed out most of the time. As we have already said, it's often ourselves and specifically our relationship with our busy lives and our stressful experiences that tend to increase our sense of busyness, frustration, anxiety and general day-to-day stress. Most busy people spend a lot of time frantically rushing around on autopilot, unaware of the varied habits that we have that are the real cause of our stress and busyness. These habits come in many forms – we have our:

- ▶ **busy story** that we tell and repeat to ourselves tirelessly and to anyone else that can bear to listen! And our

- ▶ **superhero fantasies** that we buy into and live by, which include our

- ▶ **perfectionist pursuits, habits and behaviours**, that are motivated by fear and designed (not so wisely) to eradicate all discomfort and bring about pure and everlasting peace and quiet!

If we want to feel less busy and stressed we need to start to wake up to these habitual ways of being!

> ❝*If we want to feel less busy and stressed we need to start to wake up to these habitual ways of being!*❞

We thought it could help to share another acronym at this point to help summarise how we create such a busy, unproductive and stressful and dampened-down life experience for ourselves. This is **FRANTIC**:

F Fearful (rushing around in fear, worrying that you will never get on top of everything that you need to get done).

R Reacting (reacting automatically, to every demand and request that comes your way, filling up your time with more and more things to do).

A Avoiding (trying to avoid more stress and painful feelings, by drinking more alcohol, taking drugs, disconnecting from others, daydreaming, zoning out, trying to endlessly plot and plan you next clever tactical move).

N Narrowing (narrowing your life experience, allowing all your busyness to get in the way of a rich life experience and getting on with what brings you more satisfaction and rewards).

T Trapping (trapping yourself in your busyness story, worry, problem-solving, exacerbating your cycles of stress and anxiety).

I Ignoring (neglecting your basic needs and what is really important to you in life and in any given moment).

C Careless (disconnecting from yourself and paying little careful attention to your experience).

We can remain unaware of all that we do that actually creates our sense of busyness in life. The more we rush around, the more we become increasingly FRANTIC and – as in Nick's case that follows – this lack of awareness just leads to more agitation and a growing sense of helplessness and hopelessness.

Nick

Nick was at his wits' end and run ragged when he came for mindfulness sessions. He explained that he wanted the therapy to take away all his problems. He was working all hours of the day in his painting and decorating business to ensure that he could make ends meet. He was owed money by a lot of clients, which he was furious about and his team was slacking, which he felt really aggrieved about. Further to this, two of his painters were off work with sickness and he had to keep the business ticking over, marketing to potential clients as well as do a lot more of the hands-on work himself. He spent 40 minutes of his first 50-minute session ranting about how busy he was, how unfair the situation was, how he was feeling let down, how there just wasn't enough time in the day, how exhausted he was, how his wife didn't understand his stress and how they argued a lot of the time as she thought that he was always complaining and working – and so on and on ... you get the picture! When he wasn't bleating on about all this in the session, he was either checking messages on the two mobile telephones that he had brought with him and placed next to him on the couch or actually answering calls. He clearly stated right at the ➤

---

start of this first meeting that he would have to cut the session ten minutes short as he had to attend to something urgent. Here's how some of the therapy conversation went towards the end of this first session:

Psychologist: Well, Nick, it seems that our time is now up considering that you wanted to leave earlier than we had scheduled?

Nick: What? Is that it then? You haven't even said anything, I've been doing all the talking and I don't feel any better for it at all.

Psychologist: I see, and when you think that, how do you feel?

Nick: Well, even more stressed and like I have wasted my time and still have all this to sort out.

Psychologist: Well this was indeed your time and although I am sure it seems important for you to talk about how awful everything is for you right now and that it seems crucial to you to check and answer your telephone as often as you do, I wonder if you weren't doing all that that you might feel slightly differently right now. I wonder if all that stuff was not in the way, then you may have had a different experience coming here today.

If Buddha had an iPhone ...

There's no getting away from the fact that we will feel slowed down (and annoyed) by other people and things getting in our way (or is that just us and Nick?). But we can't have the world the way we want it to be so it is better to try to accept it the way it is. Mindfulness is about changing the way we relate to our experiences, not about changing those experiences.

> " *Mindfulness is about changing the way we relate to our experiences, not about changing those experiences.* "

When you feel blocked on your way and your stress levels rise, simply noticing all the ranting that you may be doing (whether you're doing it silently to yourself or not) is a great way to come back to the present moment where there is no stress – just this one breath, this one moment. If you're stuck in a queue somewhere or waiting for a delayed train and getting stressed and angry, simply notice that reaction, you then have a choice to keep the frustration alive or do something else more productive and worthwhile with that time (sounds like a great opportunity to practise some mindfulness to us). Remember, mindfulness helps to improve our decision-making; it allows us to use our time effectively, as we base our life choices on the clarity that comes from awareness rather than from habitual reactions (such as ranting).

Next time you wake up to your ranting about being held back and delayed, how about getting mindful of your smartphone, tablet or whatever device you have to hand. We know you have one of these in some form or another – what the hell would we do without our trusty gadgets to take us away from our boredom and frustrations? The common reality is that we often become more frustrated once we have pulled them out from our pocket and been bombarded with the endless messages and emails we feel compelled to respond to – IMMEDIATELY!

Although advancements in technology are really quite astonishing, we tend to use our smartphone all day long without much thought or appreciation to the wonders of its design and the technology involved. These phones and other similar pieces of equipment have become an extension of our bodies that we tend to pay very little attention to. We use them out of habit, and the way we use and navigate through their functions has become automatic (for most of us anyway). Many of us can read and send emails, check our diaries and also send a text message to let someone know that we're too busy to be home for dinner, in the space of two minutes, without much awareness or appreciation about how we are actually doing any of this.

The purpose of the next exercise is to get acquainted with your smartphone, like you may never have before, a bit like a young child would curiously admire a present that he has just received for his birthday. It is all about reinforcing the ability that you have within yourself to break habits and act in accordance with how you wish to behave (mindfully), rather than be dictated to by some other fearful part of yourself (that may usually motivate you to constantly check your messages as soon as your phone is in sight or you're bored and frustrated being delayed somewhere). The intention of the exercise is to cultivate a non-judging awareness of your experience of your smartphone, nothing more and nothing less; to pay attention to your phone and to your experience of your touch and sight of it. Here are some pointers:

> ▶ Should any thought pop into your mind, about what you are doing, your phone (or what emails might be being pushed onto it) or anything else at all, just notice that these thoughts are there, let go of them, unhook your attention from them and bring your attention back to noticing your phone.

▶ You can do this exercise anywhere you like, such as on the train or in the back of a cab and – once you get used to it – even before and/ or after each time you use your smartphone.

▶ Remember, there is no agenda to have any particular experience of your smartphone – the only goal is to pay attention to whatever your experience is.

So with your smartphone at the ready, try this practice now. You might like to use the audio guide to assist you in this practice.

Exercise 5.1: I haven't got time for this practice

Getting acquainted with your smartphone

▶ First sit, with your smartphone on a table or other surface, on your lap in front of you or be aware of it in your pocket if you are standing up.

▶ Reach out and lift your smartphone up in your hand, notice its weight and how your hand and body is now one smartphone heavier.

▶ Next, while you hold your smartphone in hand, gently move it around, flipping it over in the palm of your hand, using your fingers, thumb and hand, notice how its weight becomes lighter and heavier on different parts of your fingers and hands.

▶ There's the weight of the smartphone and then there's you noticing its weight.

▶ Allow its weight to take centre stage in your awareness.

▶ Now, hold your smartphone still once again, allow it to rest in the palm of your hand and now run your thumb over its surface in any and all directions, notice the texture, the smoothness versus the bumps and indentations.

▶ It is natural for your attention to wander or become distracted, when this happens just gently guide it back to noticing your smartphone.

▶ Be aware that you are noticing your smartphone in this moment.

▶ There's your smartphone and then there's you noticing it and your experiences of it.

▶ Now gaze upon your smartphone, exploring it with your eyes and sight, noticing its contours, edges, colours and markings.

▶ Notice the space around your smartphone and where this space meets its edges.

▶ Notice its sleek design with wonder and curiosity.

▶ As you move your smartphone around in your hand again, notice where the light is reflected, where it shimmers and fades across its surface.

▶ Your experiences of your smartphone change – but the part of you that notices these experiences does not change, it remains pure and constant – simply aware.

▶ Should your attention wander or become distracted, just gently guide it back to noticing your smartphone.

How do you do 'busy'?

We see a lot of people come to us with expectations of how they want us to take away their problems (a bit like Nick in the above example) – they expect us to wave a magic wand and – poof – all their stress, busyness, anger and anxiety will vanish into thin air! When we hear this we just tend to hear a repetition of a habit, and we are often correct in our presumption that such an expectation prevails across all the other contexts of these people's lives – it is others that need to be different for their lives to be free from stress and busyness! As we saw from Nick's example, it's often much more to do with their own style of thinking, the scripts they tell themselves and others and the busy way that they are behaving. The lack of awareness around all of these habits and allowing all this to run on autopilot is the real reason that their stress and busyness escalates moment to moment.

Nick found it useful to ask himself the following questions, some of which you may also find helpful to think about and answer for yourself. We have added some tips for you to have a go at answering them, try this exercise now, and have a think about your answers.

Exercise 5.2: Mindfulness reflection moment

How to be a busy bee like me

▷ What is my busy-story (it's not fair, I have so much to do, others are getting in the way, etc.)?

▷ What specifically do I rant about?

▷ Does this story have any themes (focusing on past, future, failure, rejection, injustice, judging, criticising self or others)?

▷ Do I moan about how busy I am in any specific context or all contexts of my life (work, home, relationships)?

▷ What do I do when I am stressed and busy (shout, rush about, check my phone/emails, fidget, etc.)?

▷ What do others notice about me when I am busy (I am argumentative, snappy, disinterested, disconnected, accusatory, distracted, talking fast)?

▷ How do others respond to me when I am *doing* busy (comfort me, spend time with me – we guess not)?

▷ How do I respond to others when they point out my stress and busyness (tell them to shut up, they don't understand, withdraw from them)?

Exercise 5.3: Mindfulness on-the-go

Hive of busyness

Try to spend some time each day reflecting on how you do your busyness, by:

▶ Repeating the exercise above as often as you are willing to.

▶ Bringing awareness to all the habitual patterns and traps that you fall into, like your busyness script and your busy habits, behaviours and ways of being.

▶ This will help you to be more aware and to notice them as and when they arise in the future.

▶ This way you will be able to snap out of your busy habits in any given busy moment more easily and naturally.

▶ There is nothing more to do than that, awareness is the key, nothing more and nothing less – just noticing will help as it is through the moment of awareness that you can then make a choice about whether you want to continue responding the way that you were or instead make the most of that moment to move ahead in a direction that is more productive to you.

▶ By doing this exercise as often as you can you will notice that you take more satisfaction from the moment that you are actually in right there and then.

Although Nick who you met in the case example above, still had a lot to get off his chest in therapy sessions, he soon realised that there was a lot more to take from them (just like from other moments of his life), once he let go of all the busyness that he was doing and keeping alive for himself and that he was allowing to get in the way of a more fulfilling and productive experience.

Mindfulness top tips to-go

In this chapter, you have learned that it is helpful to:

▶ Pay attention to your busy automatic tendencies, such as your busy-script and busy behaviours.

▶ Engage less with this script and all the busy behaviours that you do, as your life will just feel busier and you will start to feel helpless to change it.

▶ Let go of your busy tendencies, which will free up space and energy for you to get ahead and focus your attention on more meaningful experiences in life.

CHAPTER

6

Busy doing nothing (at all helpful, anyway!)

In this chapter, we are going to turn to the thinking aspect of our stress and busyness in some more detail, here you will learn more about:

▶ How our thoughts operate and how we tend to relate to them.

▶ How we become habitually drawn to them in a particular way that only exacerbates our stress and sense of busyness in the bigger picture of our life.

▶ How mindfulness can help to develop an alternative more efficient way of being with and relating to our thoughts.

You may already, with the help of the previous chapter, have identified your particular fantasies, habitual stories and busy-bee behaviours and how these connect to your levels of stress and illusions of escape from this. So now what? We start to notice these habits using mindfulness, our awareness gradually increases, we begin to pay attention to the power of our thoughts ... so what do we do now? Surely we need to *do* something? To escape these unbearable thoughts, feelings or sensations? Want to write another to-do list then? No? Come on then, read on ... time to try something really different!

Exercise 6.1: Mindfulness reflection moment

Twinkle, twinkle, little thoughts/Now I see you now I don't

We ask that you just take a few moments before you read on:

▶ To rest in awareness as you have started to learn to do already.

▶ See if you can notice what thoughts are going through your mind as you read this right now.

▶ You might hear thoughts and your mind saying things like: *Wow this book is really quite amazing, can't wait to keep reading!* Or *What on earth are they barking on about now? Oh, do get on with it already!* Or even maybe, *They don't know what causes my stress; if only they knew how busy my life actually was they wouldn't even try to insult me with all this codswallop!*

▶ Go on, despite what your mind may be telling you, despite what thoughts may be getting in the way, try it right now for a couple of minutes, see if you can drop in to watch and notice any similar (or any different) thoughts at all going through your mind, before you read on.

Uh, uh! Why are you reading this sentence now – have you done the exercise above already? If not, do it now (you naughty thing). If so then great – so, how did you do? Did you notice any of the thoughts that showed up in your mind? If so, congratulate yourself – you were just being *mindful*! What thoughts did you notice, were they similar to the ones above?

Now, consider what impact these thoughts were having on your experience in the moment before you became aware of them: How did they make you feel? Did they affect the way you felt emotionally and/or physically? How did they help or hinder your progress in reading this book? Did they encourage you to put the book down or keep reading? Our thoughts can be very powerful when we listen to their content, they can unhelpfully affect our mood, our bodies and our behaviours and get in the way of creating the reality we want for ourselves.

We'll come back to all this a little later and you'll also get to have another go at practising mindfulness of your thoughts in some exercises that follow. But first let's have a think about all this a little more.

Letting go of worry and stressful thoughts

As we covered earlier, thoughts are part of our experience; they will come and go, passing through our awareness on their own, naturally. But what tends to happen more often when we are not being aware, is that we get caught up in our thoughts, which can have a detrimental impact on our stress levels.

❝Thoughts are part of our experience; they will come and go, passing through our awareness on their own, naturally.❞

This is what was happening to Mark as you'll discover below:

Mark

Mark, a vice-president in a large corporate bank, came for mindfulness sessions after he noticed that he was becoming increasingly anxious at work. It was the height of the credit crunch and lots of jobs were being made redundant. He had noticed how his performance at work had declined, he was unable to concentrate and was becoming increasingly more stressed and short-tempered with his team. He knew that he couldn't go on like this and feared that if his situation didn't improve he was bound to receive a bad review and might even lose his job. He had recovered from a bout of depression some two years ago and had also suffered a redundancy in a previous job in the 1990s; he didn't want to live through either experience again. Here's how some of our early conversation went:

Psychologist: What are you thinking when you're trying to get work done in the office?

Mark: Well, I never thought about my thinking before, I suppose that I'm thinking, I can't concentrate, and I can't do this! I'll never get everything done – I have so much to do! What's wrong with me? I shouldn't have made those mistakes! I am going to lose my job again!

Psychologist: How do you feel emotionally when you keep thinking 'I am going to lose my job'?

Mark: Well, I start to feel really anxious and angry.

Psychologist: OK, and what happens to you physically when you keep thinking and believing in that thought?

Mark: I start trembling, feel nauseous. It's difficult to catch my breath at times. I also get really tense; I even snapped a pen in my hand the other day out of frustration!

Psychologist: I see, and what about other thoughts, what other thoughts come off the back of thinking, 'I am going to lose my job'?

Mark: Well, I start thinking that others are laughing at me, its humiliating to be in this state. I think that I won't be able to find another job and I won't be able to enjoy what I really love to do. I think that I will have to sell my home and I have let my family down.

Psychologist: I understand, and what about your behaviour? How does your behaviour change when you keep thinking, 'I am going to lose my job'?

➤

> **Mark:** Well as I said, I get tense and can shout at my team. I sometimes rush off to the toilet to try to compose myself. I can't concentrate at all and I get no work done really! I'm useless.
>
> **Psychologist:** Well, despite the thought 'I am going to lose my job' being understandable and certainly true as a possibility, it sounds like it isn't at all helpful to keep thinking it and getting caught up in it when it pops up in your mind, especially if you want to keep your job.

We're not here to insult your intelligence and to tell you that thoughts that pop up in your mind are not true or might not happen; we're sure that you or indeed your friends and family have tried to convince you of the same. However, the questions we are encouraging you to ask yourself about any thought that shows up in your mind and that causes you stress are:

▶ Is it really *helpful* to keep thinking it?

▶ Does thinking it help you to create the reality, experience and life that you want?

▶ Does buying into this thought help you to get ahead in life?

The more we allow our minds to run on autopilot – worrying about 'catastrophic' eventualities such as losing our jobs, failing to get everything done or anything else – the more our stress levels increase and the more negative changes in our behaviour and functioning occur. In Mark's case, this makes it more likely that others will notice a drop in his performance and that job loss will inevitably follow. For Mark, paying too much attention to his worry about losing his job may have eventually become self-fulfilling.

If you think about it, like for Mark, all our stress in any moment of our life is a consequence of getting caught up in all the thoughts in our mind. These thoughts might be in the form of words in a sentence structure or images, pictures and scenarios being played out in our thinking minds. When stressed, you may be thinking about the past, regretfully, about all the things that should have happened, memories about all that went wrong. Or you may be thinking to the future, in catastrophic terms, about all that that might happen! Or you may have fantasies in your mind about how things should be; judgements, criticisms and expectations about yourself or the world around you. If you were to let go of all these thoughts, you may find that the moment you are actually in, is actually quite bearable, even quite pleasant or that something new may arise that you might not have even noticed or had the clarity of mind to act upon, if you hadn't let go of all this noise in your mind and connected to this present moment of your experience with awareness and acceptance. Just this one breath, just this moment. Mindfulness gives us this opportunity – to let go and stand back from our stressful thoughts, to truly fully appreciate this moment, just how it really is!

My life's too busy to not think!

Really? This is a common fear we hear from our busy clients, that their life is bound to fall apart if they stop thinking (there's another worrying thought to be aware of we'd say). Well, we are not here to advocate that you try to stop thinking altogether at all; in fact you'd get very frustrated and even more stressed if you tried or expected yourself to be able to. But the bottom line here is that your life wouldn't fall apart if you did stop thinking – you'd still be breathing, your heart would still be beating, you'd still be able to eat and sleep and experience much of what your life has to offer. Despite this, thinking is of course helpful, problem-solving and analysing are useful if they remain focused and productive – but there is a large difference between thinking through a problem constructively and the futility and stress that endless worry and rumination brings. Consider the following story and how sometimes no matter how many questions we ask, we may never find the answer we are looking for, and we would usually find it more helpful to just let go, accept that we may not know and get on with something more worthwhile. Ahh, freedom.

> A young child once asked his teacher, 'Teacher, what is it that holds the earth up in space?' The teacher replied, 'Oh, that would be the really large bear that holds the earth on the tip of his nose.' 'Ah, I see', replied the inquisitive child, 'but what then holds up the large bear, that holds the earth up on the tip of its nose, up in space?' 'That would be the even larger fish that holds up the bear on the tip of its fin.' 'Oh, I see teacher,' the child replied again, 'but then what holds the larger fish up, that holds the bear that holds the earth up in space?' – 'Child, it's bears and fish all the way down … .'

For many of us, as soon as we wake up, before we even open our eyes, before our feet even touch the floor, we are in stress mode, our minds racing with thoughts about the day ahead: *What do I have to get done today and how will I do that? I am going to be late! I will never get to that train in time!* Then when we are in the shower, it's not only the water but our thoughts that carry on running too, thinking about that important meeting later that day, *what will I say* and *how will others respond*, etc.? Have you ever watched an Italian football match on TV? The commentator never shuts up – oh do give it a rest, you're distracting us from the game, the main event! If you think about it now, it's probably rare that you ever really take a shower alone? You've probably got the commentator and the whole blooming football team in there with you, watching you scrub those parts that no one else can reach! What a great start to the day, hey?

It is only through awareness of your thinking that you can make decisions about how useful your thinking might be to you in any given moment.

Exercise 6.2: Mindfulness reflection moment

Think tank

Awareness of your thinking in any given moment, allows you to ask yourself, how does focusing on these thoughts …

1 Make me feel emotionally?
2 Make me feel physically?
3 Affect my behaviour?
4 Affect my relationships?
5 Interfere with my precious time?
6 Make me more efficient?
7 Help me to enjoy this moment?
8 Help me to create a satisfying life?
9 Help me to get ahead, reach my goals and what is really important to me?

Here's another quick mindfulness practice that you can try everyday (or most days we hope!) without having to change your daily routine – this time it's in the shower (or adjust accordingly if you're a bath person – either is fine). It will help you to recognise the futility of engaging with many of your thoughts as you prepare to leave the house or get ready for bed. It will allow you to get out of your head, to really enjoy your shower/bath time and wake up to the rich experience that it can be. Here're some pointers to help you get started:

- You might try to limit distractions, so turn the radio off if you usually have it on while in the shower/bath, tell others not to disturb.
- Get in the shower/bath!
- You might like to use the audio guide to assist you with this practice (don't worry, we're not really in there with you and we've seen it all before anyway, promise! Oh and please be careful, we wouldn't want to be held responsible for any incidents of electrocution!).

Exercise 6.3: I haven't got time for this practice

It's time for a scrub down!

- Notice the sound of the water as it sprays out of the shower head, as it lands on different surfaces, like your body, the tiles, shower screen or as it runs down the plug hole.
- Notice the sensation of water, its pressure hitting against your head, your different body parts; the temperature of the water against your body. Notice how this feels.
- Notice the smell of the soap and the shampoo.
- Notice how the soap and shampoo feel against your skin, and how it feels as it washes away.
- Notice the water droplets on the walls or shower screen and dripping down your body.
- Notice the steam rising and filling the shower, the room.
- Should any thoughts show up about what you are doing, or anything else at all, just acknowledge these thoughts, let go of them and bring your attention back to your experience of the shower.
- Who would have guessed that without all those thoughts crowding in with you (maybe about the boss/car mechanic/David Cameron), that your shower could be so spacious!

Stop with the positives!

Mark, who we met earlier, exhaled a great sigh of relief when he thought that all he had to do was focus less on certain unhelpful thoughts to get rid of his distress. However he soon realised that this was a lot harder to do than it sounded or than he had first presumed. The truth is that Mark's situation was stressful and he would understandably feel anxious and have worrying thoughts about it – there's no getting away from that fact. Mark's attempts to get rid of his stressful thoughts by trying to think positively, like, *I am not going to lose my job*, or to distract his attention away from his worrying thoughts, by *thinking* about something else when these sorts of thoughts showed up, were just not working to bring about the outcome he expected – to stop his thoughts and get rid of his distress. His worrying thoughts just kept popping back up and he continued to feel more and more upset. See, Mark was actually still caught up in these thoughts, either by thinking the opposite/positive in relation to them or distracting himself from them – either way he still had them in mind (and he felt the stress and tension in his body too), in his struggle with them.

Patterns in the mind

Neuroscience helps us to understand that our brains actually create networks of thoughts (neurological connections and pathways), one thought is associated with another; so one thought may ignite further thoughts (there is no black without white, see what we mean?), a story or script if you like. Much like a computer we hold these programmes or networks in mind but, very much unlike a computer, we can't delete these programmes ever. So what can we do if certain thoughts and stories are stressing us out? Well we can stop strengthening the programme or thinking network that is causing us stress, we can wake up to when we are thinking it, see it for what it is – just a thought, a story (rather than listening to the content of it and then trying to do something about it) – and therefore stop reinforcing it. Once we do this, we can put our attention into creating a whole new and more helpful programme and network of thoughts. Simple (but not so easy, it's a discipline that needs to be practised, and we'll show you how very soon).

Exercise 6.4: Mindfulness reflection moment

Tying yourself in (k)nots

This simple exercise is intended to amuse and, more importantly, to show you how all your hard work spent trying to get rid of thoughts and feelings by trying to think positively or by trying to distract yourself from them is never going to pay off. Try really, really hard at the following tasks:

▶ Don't think of a pink elephant with black and yellow spots.

▶ Think of the dog/cat/goldfish/mother-in-law dying – feel nothing.

▶ Think of winning the lottery – feel nothing, do not imagine what you could do with the cash.

▶ Recall an incident where you could've said something witty and clever, berate yourself endlessly and now turn to the person nearest to you and say something witty and clever.

▶ Look in the mirror and have no negative thoughts at all, ever again.

▶ Do not think about how stressful this exercise is, when you have so many more important things to do.

Like you, Mark certainly didn't need a psychologist to tell him to think positively or to distract himself; he had tried all that before anyway. He needed a new strategy – and that's where mindfulness helped him.

Short circuiting the thinking mind

The truth is that we might not be able to stop thoughts popping into our mind but we certainly have a choice about what kind of attention we give to them when they do. If you had the thought, *I am a green alien from outer space*; the chances are that you would laugh that thought off without paying any real attention to it at all (we assume, but if you do have this thought and don't find yourself laughing it off, that's OK too). But, like Mark, if you noticed a thought that presented some threat to your downfall in life, suggesting something about your failure or rejection in some area of your life – such as *I am fat, I am ugly, I will never get all this done today, I am going to lose my job* – then you'd be more likely to pay lots of attention to it. This attention is motivated by our inherent survival mechanism (see Chapter 4 to refresh yourself on this), which is programmed to believe that if we don't pay attention to the threat (content of that thought) and try to work it out somehow then it is bound to get worse and lead to our downfall.

It may surprise you to know that you have the power within you to treat any thought that may show up in your mind in the same way that you would treat the thought *I am a green alien from outer space,* which is a really helpful ability if certain thoughts are causing you stress and getting in the way of what you want to achieve in life. You simply don't have to pay attention to or think the thoughts in your mind if you choose not to. Wow! Amazing! We know, right? *Well how do I do that?* we hear you ask. Well, you know the drill by now, before we take a look at how we can develop more of the ability to stand back from our stressful thoughts, let's just take a moment to gain a better understanding of how our minds work by taking a closer look at the amazing world that goes on in our heads.

The hamster mind

As we mentioned in the previous section, we have two modes of our mind: the *thinking mind* and the *awareness mind.* This book is all about getting more in touch with our *awareness mind* and cultivating the ability to drop into it more often when we choose; as it is when in this mode of mind that we can practise mindfulness, reap all the associated benefits to our mood and well-being and truly appreciate life just how it is.

We now want to encourage you to consider your thinking mind as a very busy hamster, frantically and endlessly running on its wheel. Because what is also certain about our thinking mind is that it is a creature of habit, reinforcing its same pattern of busy behaviour throughout our lives. Close your eyes and imagine your wee furry friend right now, so cute and adorable, gnawing away constantly at all those worries and problems. Give them a peanut for all their hard work as we now explore our hamster mind a little more.

Creatures of habit – understanding your hamster

Our hamster (thinking) mind is on autopilot in very much the same way as the many other habits that we tend to find ourselves running through automatically each day, such as our morning ablutions, our journey to and from work, rushing around to get everything done, etc. Much like the varied behaviours that make up these daily tasks, there is also a pattern of intricate and connecting thoughts (patterns of thoughts as we saw above) that occur in our thinking minds that we remain mostly unaware of as they continue to tick away on autopilot each day. Our thinking mind is a problem-solver – much like a hamster, busy doing, analysing, trying to reach the end of its wheel, trying to find an end result and work everything out.

Now as we have said, this problem-solving habit of the thinking mind is all very good when we have a practical problem to solve, such as how do we get from A to B. In fact, without the problem-solving habit of the thinking mind we might never have learned how to get ourselves dressed as a child, been able to find our way to and from work as an adult or sniff out the tastiest seeds as a hamster. This problem-solving approach to our lives is forever reinforced amidst our busy days, and also often within the technical aspects of our work. It helps us to navigate ourselves through the entirety of tasks to get things ticked off on our to-do lists (yes, those again!) often with much success. It is quite understandable therefore that when we have an emotional problem (like Mark in the earlier example), that we would instinctively apply the same tried-and-tested problem-solving approach to navigate our way out of it – we feel the need to evaluate it, to understand where this problem has come from, where is it going, what you need to prepare yourself for in the face of it. This is completely understandable and natural (but usually unhelpful).

As we saw, Mark's instinctive tendency to think his way through his emotional problem in this way just seemed to escalate and worsen it even more – his thinking mind wasn't helping him to resolve his situation (emotional 'problem') at all – he just became more anxious and irritable as a result. When he noticed his mood worsen and his functioning and behaviour decline, in true testament to this thinking mind, he begun to ruminate and worry on past negative experiences, what had been going wrong, all that he could not do, and what negative eventualities might materialise and where this all might end up for him once again. As he thought through his problem in this way his mood and performance deteriorated. Imagine your hamster, running faster on the wheel, perhaps believing that the cat is coming, but running faster to escape is not the answer!

Living by the cause and effect rule

When we feel some discomfort – whether that be physically or emotionally – our instinctive problem-solving approach/thinking mind pipes up automatically, working hard to 'protect' us. The hamster will defend us, the mighty beast! This is our attempt to understand the problem as we see it, to prevent it from getting worse by ensuring we know what eventualities we need to prepare ourselves for and generally to lessen its impact on our lives and hopefully resolve it. We think in terms of cause and effect – why and how did this happen and what will happen as a result.

Now of course, the more we think in terms of the past and the future, both in terms of the worst, berating ourselves for our past mistakes, remembering our difficulties and worrying about the worst to come, the more we actually come to experience the emotional impact of all these thoughts in the very present moment of doing so – exacerbating the emotional distress and associated physical and behavioural consequences as a result – this is exactly what Mark found himself doing when thinking about his anxiety and behaviour in this way.

We have an astonishing ability to look into the past and to predict our future, but this is all too often to our own detriment.

Our problem-solving mind is not going to solve an emotional 'problem' no matter how hard it tries – emotions aren't a problem to be solved, they are a condition of life and therefore they do not have a solution. We have an astonishing ability to look into the past and to predict our future, but this wonderful tool is all too often to our own detriment (like many of the other tools that we have created for ourselves over the centuries, that have all served their purpose at one time or another, feel free to discard and drop this one too, if it's not working well for you). The habitual behaviour of our hamster minds is in fact the real problem that we have to deal with.

Watching thoughts come and go

Touching a thought that pops up into our thinking mind with awareness is like touching a soap bubble, the emotional impact of the thought *vanishes*. The simple and beautiful reality is that we cannot be both in our thinking mode of mind (running on our hamster wheel) and our awareness mode of mind (noticing the hamster frantically running) at the same time – it's humanly impossible. In other words, as soon as we 'wake up' and notice that our hamster is frantically running around its wheel, we simultaneously stop the hamster in its tracks – it's all about where and how we choose to focus our attention. With each moment of awareness of your thoughts, the negative thinking spiral is broken and the thinking mind's habit is not reinforced.

Mark, who we met in the earlier case example, who was feeling anxious at work, thought that this all sounded great but asked what he should do with the thought once he had noticed it. As we have outlined, *NOTHING*, that's it – noticing is all we have to do. We are so programmed in a way to do something that it is understandable that, like Mark, we feel a bit weird about doing nothing and believe that surely there is something else that needs to be done. Remember you are cultivating a totally new way of being and relating to your experience and specifically your thoughts in this instance, it will feel unusual at first. Doing something more will only lead you down the same problematic path of analysing and struggling once again.

So, simply noticing and becoming aware of our thoughts, rather than trying to challenge them with positive thoughts or push them out altogether is the way that we gain relief from the stress and emotional impact of our thoughts. Quite contrary to our usual attempts to get rid of thoughts and their associated feelings, what we are actually doing with awareness of our thoughts, is holding and noticing these same thoughts (as they are, just thoughts, not listening to their content) and the feelings that arise from them, in our attention. While we are doing this we lose the emotional impact of them in that moment – we are not exacerbating them or making them worse – instead we are noticing and accepting them for what they are (thoughts, stories, sounds, images, experiences in our mind). Furthermore, we are freeing up the natural tendency for our thoughts to come and then to pass by of their own accord as they naturally will. We now have abundant space with which to experience and actually live our lives, in this very moment, allowing us to get on with, savour and gain greater pleasure from what is worthwhile and fulfilling to us, like enjoying our shower!

Back away from the brick wall

With mindfulness we are able to stand back, distance and disconnect ourselves from the content of our thoughts, and see them exactly for what they are – streams of words, sentences, images, pictures or events in our mind, passing by in our awareness. As we have seen, what we instinctively and usually do is get caught up in them and what they may somehow be telling us and assume that they represent some real danger or threat. We might find ourselves scurrying through these thoughts and images like Mystic Meg looking into her tea leaves, attempting to glean portends about the future; no matter how compelling this seems, it is about as effective as trying to dig yourself out of a hole. Save yourself the trouble of consulting an old quack (your thoughts) and let them drift off into the ether. You don't need to waste so much energy figuring 'it all' out – this is really stressful for you and it doesn't work well anyway. And as hard and tricky as it seems to resist meddling in your thoughts and instead to distance yourself from them, the pay-off is that after all these years of banging your head against a brick wall you finally notice how painful it's been and that you have a headache – plus you are still no closer to 'the answer'. Now, you know, and we've already told you there is no answer, so back away from the wall and see how much of a relief it is to let go of it all.

Exercise 6.5: Mindfulness on-the-go

Seeing your thoughts as if they were ...

▶ To help you distance yourself from thoughts you can try to imagine that they are the voices of some noisy school children playing up in the back of the car, shouting abuse and judgements at you, as you drive them to school. They may be shouting: *you're going the wrong way – you'll never get us to school on time.* Your natural tendency may be to slam your foot onto the brake and turn around to the children and tell them to be quiet and argue back: *I know exactly where I am going and we will be there in good time.* Of course, the more you do that, the more fuel you are adding to the fire, encouraging them to argue back with you some more. Instead, what you *can* do is keep your foot on the accelerator and your eyes on the road ahead of you, ignoring the abuse that you can hear although remaining aware of it in the back of the car, and eventually, soon enough the children (your unhelpful thoughts) will quieten down, leaving you free to pursue and efficiently complete you task of getting them to school on time (or whatever your goal in reality may be).

▶ You may also try to imagine that your thoughts are like the sound coming from the radio as you are busy getting on with the housework, or some other task at work. So, if someone asked you what the radio show was all about, you may reply that, although you heard that it was on in the background, you didn't pay much attention to it at all.

▶ You could imagine that you are standing at the side of a busy city road and that your thoughts are all the taxis whizzing past you – just remember as you stand there watching them in this way not to jump into the back of one to catch a ride.

▶ Another metaphor is to imagine yourself like a mountain – perhaps even feeling this in your body, standing firm, solid and steady. The thoughts come like the weather ... rain, sunshine, snow, gentle breezes and howling gales; the seasons and weather systems come and go and still the mountain remains, true and steady.

▶ A busy mind could also be considered like a handful of coloured helium balloons, or a flock of birds chattering in a tree, ready to rise one by one, or all together into the skies.

▶ Thoughts forming can sometimes be released, almost to dissolve, on an out breath, which is a natural process of letting go (see Chapter 3 to remind you about mindful breathing).

▶ You could also imagine that there are leaves floating down a flowing stream in front of you and that each time a stressful thought shows up in your mind that you place that thought on one of the leaves and watch it float away.

Yes, we know we have probably gone into overdrive with this metaphor-thing by now (we noticed that too and enjoyed a chuckle together about it). We want to give you all we have got, to make sure that this book works, is relevant and engaging for as many people as possible – yes, we want to get it perfect and right! Do we leave them in or delete them – oh Michael, I don't know? Josie, what should we do? Told you we were just like you, fearful (of our failings and rejection – our downfall) like the next man or woman. We don't know the answer either. Mindfulness doesn't tell us whether we are 'right' or 'wrong'. Too many metaphors? No answer except some birds tweeting (squawk).

▶ You may also like to label your thoughts as they show up in your mind throughout the day – you may silently say to yourself: *thinking* to allow yourself to stand back from them and notice them for what they really are – just events, sounds, images passing through your awareness.

▶ You may even like to try labelling them more specifically, for example if you notice that you are regretfully thinking over the past you may silently say to yourself: *past*, or if you are worry about the future: *future*. If at another time, you notice that you are giving yourself a hard time or judging and evaluating yourself or others, simply label this thinking as: *criticism/judgement* in that very moment to ensure that you remain present rather than flapping away to some other time and place along with that squawking flock of birds!

With all these ways of seeing and responding to your thoughts it is important to recognise that your thoughts may come and go, they may change, become louder or quieter, show up more frequently or infrequently but while all this is happening in your thinking mind, your awareness of them does not change. It can hold these thoughts in awareness while your attention (awareness) expands to also focus on whatever task you want to get on with instead. If, on the other hand, you allow your attention to get caught up in thoughts, maybe analysing or struggling with the content of what they are saying, don't be surprised if you end up in a place that you don't want to be in at all – you'll be on the first fast train out of here, straight to stress-ville (but that's OK also, because there are no one-way tickets to anywhere when it comes to mindfulness)!

Exercise 6.6: Mindfulness on-the-go

Mindfulness of thoughts – the thinking person's brain

As you did at the start of this chapter, have another go at reinforcing your ability to watch your thoughts with this exercise right now and as you are on the go. Just follow the simple steps outlined below:

1 Freeze right now.
2 Watch your thoughts arise in your mind for one minute (don't count the time just take a rough guess at how long a minute is while you do this).
3 Notice your thoughts.
4 No need to stop your thoughts.

5 Let your thoughts come, see them go, use one of the metaphors or labelling techniques from above, to help you do this.

You may have noticed some similar thoughts to *I'm too busy to do this* or *What a load of tosh* or *I feel stupid* or *This is a really long minute* or *What would my boss say if s/he knew I was doing this?* or *I feel so chilled – this is it!* or *Been doing this for ten seconds and it still isn't working* or *What shall I have for tea?* or anything else at all.

These are some of our thoughts as we write this book right now (we're not telling whose is whose though!!):

It is stuffy in here, My feet ache, What can I write in the book that sounds really brilliant?, I'm not doing this properly, Would someone switch that bloody music off I'm trying to work here!, We'll never get this book written in time for the deadline, Ahh, welcome my little monkey mind, Breathing, Hungry.

❝Remember this is a drastically different way of being from usual, that will come with patience and practice.❞

If you find this hard or don't notice any thoughts, don't be concerned, discouraged or give up, just give the exercise another go when you have a few minutes to spare. Remember this is a drastically different way of being from usual, that will come with patience and practice.

Exercise 6.7: Mindfulness on-the-go

Stepping off the hamster wheel back into reality

Along with noticing and labelling your thoughts as outlined above, throughout your day and when you feel stressed, you might like to try to create more space between you and your thoughts by using either (or both) of the following two techniques.

First, you could try repeating any of your stressful thoughts that show up in your mind, with a few words added before each of them. These few 'mindful' words are:

I notice the thought that …

Mark in the example earlier, tried this technique with the worry that showed up in his mind about his stressful work situation. When at work and feeling stressed, he would take a few moments to notice the thoughts whizzing through his mind and repeat them using this technique. For Mark it sounded like this:

> *I notice the thought that I am going to lose my job.*

Try it now with these steps

1 Think of a thought that stresses you out, it might be: *I am never going to get all this stuff done in time*, or the like.

2 Spend a moment or two thinking your stressful thought, silently repeating it to yourself in your mind, really believing it.

3 Notice how stressed you can feel as a result of buying into and believing this thought.

4 Now, repeat the thought but this time add those few '*mindful*' words before it, so it might sound like: *I notice the thought that I am never going to get this stuff done in time* (or whatever your stressful thought was). Repeat the thought with these added few words before it, a few times silently.

5 Notice what happens – did you feel any sense of distance between you and your stressful thought? Did your level of stress change at all? (Remember if it did, this is just a fortunate by-product of using this mindful, awareness and acceptance of thoughts technique.)

Second, along with the above technique you might like to try another, which is all about repeating your stressful thoughts rapidly and silently to yourself. When we do this the thought turns into a sound, it loses its content and meaning, and we come to notice just a sound in our mind. Remember that's all a thought ever was – a sound in your mind, and if you listen too much to its content you allow that sound to determine how you feel emotionally and physically and how you behave. Try this now, to see what we mean.

▶ Repeat the word (thought) *MILK*, over and over again quickly, silently in your mind.

▶ Notice what happens …

▶ It just becomes a sound, right?

These techniques really help to wake us up in any given moment to the fact that we might be running on autopilot in our thinking minds, replaying stressful thoughts over and over again and worsening our stressed mood. It helps us to connect to the present moment of reality again and again and realise that right now, in this moment, I am noticing something, an experience and event in my mind, called a thought, running through my thinking mind, and in paying too much attention to the content of this thought I am affecting my reality. The result is that we immediately stand back from our thinking mind and step instead into our awareness mind and simultaneously lose any of the emotional impact that our thinking mind might be having on us in that very moment. We also free up time, energy and space to move forwards with what is more important to us.

When using these techniques, it may only be one second (or less!) before your thinking mind pipes up once again to replay the stressful thought (or another one) and captures your attention with it once again, and that is OK. All you have to do is repeat one of the techniques above. It's important to remember that these techniques are not designed to stop the stressful thoughts occurring, or to make them occur less frequently or to make you feel less stressed (these are just fortunate by-products and outcomes, should they occur). Instead the purpose of these techniques and your goal in using them is to simply connect to the present moment, to cultivate as much awareness of your thinking mind as you can in that very moment of stress. In every moment of awareness that comes with using these techniques you can be confident to know that you will no longer be reinforcing the habits of the 'thinking mind'. Instead, you are now developing the strength of your 'awareness mind', increasing the likelihood that you will more naturally bring awareness to future moments of stress, freeing up more time and energy.

Finally, it may be helpful (oh no, not another metaphor) to think of yourself like a benevolent Barbara Woodhouse (a famous old dog trainer), training your unruly mind, effervescent as a puppy, to heel by connecting mindfully with the present moment. So as you go about your busy days, just try to notice your thoughts and remember who's meant to be taking who for a walk; is it you taking your mind or is your mind taking you!?

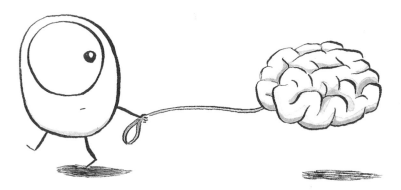

Exercise 6.8: Mindfulness on-the-go

Hey thoughts, I see you!

As you move about your busy day:

▶ Try to notice your thoughts as much as you can.

▶ Remember, you don't have to carve any special time out of your day to do this.

▶ Just simply go about your normal busy day-to-day stuff, but with the purpose and intention that you will bring more awareness to your thoughts.

▶ Try to notice all and any thoughts, both the upsetting and less upsetting ones.

▶ Remember you are trying to cultivate as much awareness as you can, so this is not only an exercise to practise on thoughts that are causing you stress.

▶ Just silently note and acknowledge them as they arise, maybe labelling them, *thinking*, and see if you can label the type of thinking that has occurred, like *that's worry*, or *that's analysing*, or *past, future, judgement, criticism*, etc., or use the techniques above (*I notice the thought that …*) and then carry on with your day.

▶ The more you practise this the more you will find that you naturally and instinctively bring more awareness to thoughts at stressful times. You will be better able to stop your hamster in its tracks and lessen the emotional impact of it at inevitable stressful times in your life.

The techniques described in this chapter are designed to help you cultivate more awareness of your *thoughts* and are to be used as often and for however long you wish. We assure you that you will not have to use them all the time, indefinitely (although they may be helpful to pull out of your self-help 'tool-kit' from time to time when you are feeling particularly stressed out and busy – we know we still use them often; they can work a treat when we notice we are all too caught up in our thinking mind and choose to get back to reality). They are designed to help you get started, like stabilisers on your first bike, and in time you will be bringing awareness to your thoughts more instinctively and naturally. As you continue to practise, the most important thing to remember is that with practising mindfulness of thoughts you are not trying to think positively or stop thinking at all, you are simply becoming more aware of your thoughts – noticing them. Nothing more and nothing less than that.

In the next section we are going to take a closer look at the other aspects of our stress and busyness – our feelings and body sensations. Also, in doing so you are going to discover what it is that exactly lies beneath all the day-to-day busyness you experience and more about how your way of responding to this is what is really keeping you so busy. Ready?

Well, hold your horses for a moment, as we want to end this chapter and section of the book leaving you with one more mindfulness practice that you can no doubt fit into any day, probably more than once. It's also a great one to help you get out of your head and into your daily, present moment experience as you rush around from here to there ... it's all about *walking mindfully*.

Most of us tend to walk around on autopilot while our minds are usually caught up in thoughts about all the things we need to do or places we need to get to. How often do you walk a familiar route (whether that be outdoors or from your bed to the bathroom or even across the office floor) only to arrive at your destination realising you have noticed nothing along the way? How aware are you of your body and your surroundings when you walk? Have you ever really noticed the amazing intricacies and functionality of your body? We just walk automatically, never really noticing or appreciating the splendid design and ability that our bodies have. In the next exercise, we are going to bring awareness to the experience of walking, in the present moment.

- ▶ Try this whenever you can, as often as you can.
- ▶ Even if it's only on a short walk from your bed to the bathroom first thing in the morning, across the office floor during the day, or even to and from the canteen or train station each day.
- ▶ Rushing from one place to the next may never feel the same again.
- ▶ You might like to use the audio guide to assist you in this practice.

Exercise 6.9: I haven't got time for this practice

Walkies!

▶ As you begin to walk, first notice the sensation in your feet against the ground.

▶ Notice the automatic process and impulse of moving your legs. One leg rising and protruding forward to take the first step, then the next leg ready to follow with the second step.

▶ Notice the automatic impulses and movements in your arms.

▶ Notice what muscles tense or relax as you move your body to this thing we call walking.

▶ Acknowledge the weight of your body shifting between your left and right hip, your left and right leg, as you walk.

▶ Notice how you are stepping, the quality of each step (whether you are stepping hard or lightly onto the ground), and the feel of your feet within your shoes, and the ground beneath your feet.

▶ Become aware of the sensations of the air against your skin as you propel forwards. Notice the difference in sensations between areas that are exposed to the air and areas that are covered by clothes.

▶ How does the material of your clothing move against your skin as you walk?

▶ Expand your awareness to notice your surroundings.

▶ As you walk, what do you see, smell, hear, taste and feel?

▶ What do you notice around you? If this is a familiar walk, what do you notice that you never have before?

▶ Expand your awareness so that you remain aware of the sensations of walking and the external environment while you also become aware of your internal experiences, such as your thoughts and emotions.

▶ What thoughts cross your mind as you walk?

▶ What emotions are there right now? Are they intense, or mild?

▶ Are these internal experiences pulling you in or can you observe them with a little bit of distance?

▶ No need to judge these internal experiences as good or bad, practise just noticing them for what they are.

▶ If at any point during your walk you notice your mind wandering to the past or the future, or being pulled away from your experience of walking, just gently acknowledge that your mind has wandered and bring yourself back to the present moment and the walk.

▶ Remember that being pulled away and coming back is the key to mindfulness practice.

Right, so chapter finished, well done for staying with it. Here's your top tips to go, as promised.

Mindfulness top tips to-go

In this chapter you have learned that it is helpful to:

▶ See how powerful thoughts can be and how they can have an unhelpful impact on our stress levels.

▶ Try not to get caught up in unhelpful thoughts, it's futile, time-consuming, makes us inefficient and leads us away from reaching our goals and the life we want.

▶ Understand the habitual behaviour of your hamster mind.

▶ Try not to think positively or distract yourself in the face of stressful thoughts, struggling with them like this just makes us more stressed and is time-consuming.

▶ Stand back, be more mindful and bring more awareness to your thoughts.

▶ Use specific techniques to notice your thoughts (rather than always reinforcing the stressful networks and patterns in your thinking mind) and to reduce stress.

▶ Connect to your present life experience to get out of your head and back to enjoying your reality.

Part 2 summary

In this second part of the book we have taken a closer look at what the real cause and maintaining factor of our stressful and busy lives is, we have looked at the connection between stress and busyness and how we might be better able to manage some of the specific experiences of our stress, including our thoughts, and behaviours with mindfulness. More specifically, you have learned that:

▶ A stress-free existence is an illusion.

▶ Chasing this illusion is futile and only creates more stress and busyness.

▶ We create a greater sense of stress and busyness for ourselves.

▶ We miss out on such a varied and wonderful experience in life when we are consumed by busyness (our habitual stories, thoughts, behaviours), dampening down our rich life experience.

▶ We don't have to change a thing or be less busy to create a sense of more time for ourselves.

▶ We are programmed a certain way, due to our primeval ancestors – that's the way it is, we need to wake up to this primitive quality or we run the risk of burnout and high levels of distress.

▶ Our thoughts affect our mood, sensations and behaviours and listening to the content of unhelpful thoughts is the cause of much of our distress.

In the next part of the book we are going to assist you by:

▶ Furthering your exploration and practice of mindfulness.

▶ Introducing you to some more practical techniques and exercises and helpful insights regarding your emotions and physical aches and pains.

We hope you enjoy it, as much as we have enjoyed writing it!

Part

3

Mindfulness and difficult emotions

How to fall in the muck gracefully

From the previous parts of this book we can now see how our thoughts:

▶ are a 'product' of the mind, fleeting experiences that come and go;

▶ contribute to the busyness of our lives when we get caught up in them;

▶ take up a lot of attention if we allow them to and then make us less efficient; and

▶ are responsible for perpetuating a LOT of stress.

We also know now, how this is all related to our caveman (or cave-woman) tendencies, so we can drop the guilt about being like this and blame our prehistoric ancestors. So, when we let go of the thoughts, stop trying to think positively, and stop distracting ourselves with them – what do we find? What are we *really* avoiding and trying to get away from? What is all this busy rushing around in aid of, what's our purpose with it? When we take a look by stepping out of and noticing our thinking mind, allowing it to naturally slow, still or recede, then up pop the emotions.

In the following section of this book we are going to look specifically at difficult emotions. Sometimes, emotions can be tricky little blighters and often they are a bit uncomfortable. Imagine a really great party… you're having a good time, checking out the babes, drinking your Babycham – and then you realise that you have socks *and* sandals on at the same time! You smell of garlic! Your hair has mysteriously all fallen out! Everyone knows what you did last summer! And you can see all the geeks coming your way waving and shouting your name! Argh! Yep – that's the kind of party we're talking about. Perhaps, you would normally turn and run, but as we know this is what we always do, in fact, this is just like our busy hamster mind whirring away to try and find solutions, but actually we are just creating more problems in our frantic efforts to avoid difficult, painful feelings. In honour of this we will consider these difficult emotions to be frequently thought of as 'the party poopers of mindfulness'; just when it was all going so well, we were having a nice time and then along come these little stinkers. Our experience and struggle with these difficult emotions is often the very cause of our busyness. Also they can be the most common reasons why we believe that we cannot practise mindfulness itself, we tell ourselves it's not 'working' and can feel like giving up.

When most of us first try mindfulness, we can often find a sense of tranquillity and restfulness which is very pleasant – the party is good and it's pretty nice. Sometimes, if we don't, we believe that we 'should' be finding it tranquil and restful and are frustrated either at the world around us or at ourselves for making this experience something else. These can be quite superficial things like *I can't sit still when I have so much to do right now*, *If only I hadn't worn these socks and sandals, then I could concentrate*, *I'm too tired or stressed right now* or *If I was more comfy I would be able to do mindfulness*; sometimes our resistance is deeper like *I am too sad to practise* or *I am failing at this*. We may also deeply feel that we have no right to ever really be happy so we don't even give ourselves a fair chance of this either and as such life becomes dull, numb and grey as we try to avoid feeling anything and just distract ourselves continually with endless tasks. Of course, ironically this is actually very painful indeed and often leads to depression. Alternatively we think we will be overwhelmed with emotions, perhaps we are scared of 'going mad' or being exposed as weak or vulnerable that we need to run away from life and hide in a cupboard. This is all very common.

> **❝We do not need to be still, quiet, peaceful or even happy to be mindful. ❞**

The truth is that actually we do not *need* to be still, quiet, peaceful or even happy to be mindful. We do not need to try to stop being so busy either.

Mindfulness on-the-go

Awareness is with you all the time

Over the next week, no matter how busy you are in any given moment, whatever you are doing, wherever you are, try to make a purposeful effort to:

▷ Drop into your awareness and notice your emotions.
▷ Notice that you are aware and noticing your emotions.
▷ It just takes a second to notice and to notice that you are noticing.

Let's have a go at this right now so you know what we mean:

▷ Notice how you're feeling emotionally right now (happy, excited, bored, frustrated, stressed).
▷ Acknowledge the fact that you are noticing your emotions.

So over the next week (and thereafter) keep noticing your emotions (the 'good' and the 'bad' ones) and the fact that you are noticing them. You may notice how you feel when:

- You speak to your colleague at work, partner at home, etc.
- You rush around walking from here to there.
- You catch sight of a stunning cherry tree from the window of the bus as the drivers change shifts.
- You hear the sound of the water boiling in the kettle as you make a quick cup of tea.
- You're sitting at your desk at work.

Remember once you notice these feelings (or whatever you notice), also notice/acknowledge that you have noticed them.

We are not trying to sell you a brand new cleaning product that will eliminate 99.9% of all difficult emotional germs, so that life will be sterilised and never contaminated with any mucky stuff again. This would be like selling you snake oil; it would be a con. In fact by planting even the seed of such a hope for a life free from the stain of difficult emotions you might find yourself trying to forget about the difficult emotions all together and look for something different – like getting on with all the work you have to do by rushing to fit it all into your day – and that *is* going to create *more* difficult emotions.

This part of the book is all about waking up to the reality of difficult and sometimes painful emotions, which, in all amazement, brings with it such a fantastic sense of relief, clarity, productivity and well-being. You will also learn:

- To notice your busyness whatever you are doing.
- To understand that you do not need to run away from difficult emotions, and that running away actually makes things more difficult.
- To find ways of understanding what lies beneath your busyness.
- To accept difficult emotions as part of life, to realise you can actually cope with them and that this releases a lots of energy, productivity and mental clarity to help us to get ahead in life.
- To recognise that you can continue to be busy and actually increase your effectiveness, efficiency and sense of ease when mindful of your difficult emotions.

What lies beneath all the busyness?

So we think we have come through loud and (hopefully) clear by now – the less busy we try to become the busier we may find that we actually are! But even with this realisation and all our attempts to remain aware of our habitual busy tendencies, we may still find ourselves frantically rushing around like a headless chicken a lot of the time. Firstly, we want to say, that's OK, Rome wasn't built in a day now, was it? And remember you are learning a drastically new way of being – a new habit! However, it might be helpful to understand a little more about what is going on beneath all this busyness that most of us busy people do a lot of the time without even realising we are doing it.

Mindfulness highlights our life's habits and patterns that keep us in a confusing maze of distress that we struggle to 'work out' or fix. When we can't seem to do this, either we tell ourselves that we are failing, others are failing us or our environment is failing us. We then struggle with our 'superhero' complex (see Chapter 2) – we either expect ourselves to be omnipotent, omniscient and akin to a god, perfectly in control and indomitable (which causes a great deal of isolation from others and is rather grandiose) or we are basically a kind of scum, weak, idiotic and worthless. Well, whether it is the thought that we are wearing the wrong clothes to a party or a centrally held certainty that we are not good enough, with mindfulness we can learn to let go, to steady the mind, to ease into the present moment and to gradually release ourselves from the grip of these mental stories that keep us so very busy.

In this chapter we are going to help you discover:

▶ How your emotions and busyness are linked.

▶ What emotions lay beneath your busyness.

▶ What you can 'do' in response to those emotions.

▶ How you can be less busy and stressed by transforming your relationship with your emotions.

Our wired world

Initially recognising our painful emotions can be tricky, as every cell in our bodies goes on 'red alert'. As you will recall from Part 2, our cortisol levels rise (we feel we are under threat), we feel stressed by trying so hard to figure out just what to 'do' about it all to make it all stop and go away. We bump into our difficult emotions and try to 'fix' them, preferably really quickly, because they don't feel nice, both physically and mentally. The more we keep going and struggling like this, the worse the feelings get, until often we do end up giving up. We see this in our clinic every day. The case study below highlights such an instance. Rita, perhaps just like you, struggled with the counterintuitive idea that if we just stop trying so hard to fix everything then life becomes much simpler and we are much more effective. The strength of this pattern nearly led her to quit therapy (like so many other things she'd tried so hard with but still felt like she was 'failing'). Instead she realised that there was nothing to fail, because this wasn't a test, or an appraisal, or a kind of trick – there wasn't really anything at all to fix, figure out or mend.

Rita

Rita was an attractive, successful and intelligent young woman who worked as a management consultant in the city. She had always worked diligently and unceasingly to overcome her 'flaws' and manage her 'deficits'. She did this at work, in her relationships and even questioned the very core of her personality. She came to therapy seeking another answer to her problems, looking for strategies, and techniques to cure her depressed mood and persistent feelings of failure. Her expectation for dealing with her difficult emotions was to look at what therapy could do about them, to get rid of them and she was prepared to work very hard to make them go away.

She took out her notebook to write out her to-do list from the session and found the explanation that this was not going to work quite shocking.

This is an excerpt from a session, discussing her difficult emotion of loneliness. She is asked to do nothing about it, just to breathe mindfully, to notice her thoughts and physical sensations arising. It went something like this:

Breathing in: tension in the solar plexus.

Breathing out: overwhelmed with feeling of loneliness.

Breathing in: *This is unbearable; I have to make it stop*.

Breathing out: tightness in the chest.

Breathing in: feelings of panic.

Breathing out: *I can't do this*.

Breathing in: *I need to make it stop*.

➤

She stops the practice, exclaiming she can't do mindfulness. She is crying. She is encouraged that she has got it! But she doesn't understand. She is absolutely right; she can't 'do' mindfulness. She has just discovered her habitual pattern, the one that is the real cause of so much distress. She is noticing all those thoughts exclaiming to her that she 'can't cope' and she is believing them, and wanting desperately to act on them by 'doing' something. Because this response to her difficult emotions is so habitual for her and she is such a high achiever, she has attributed her success to her busyness and her failure to not trying hard enough. This has meant Rita has become busier and tried harder even when it hasn't been working. As a consequence her performance at work actually declined, she was depressed, anxious and working longer and longer hours with no time for her relationship, friends or pleasure. In fact, when Rita learned that she could be just as busy without grasping at success and running away from failure her anxiety and depression left, she had a successful relationship, felt happier and became more productive, confident and efficient at work.

Emotions are a condition, not a problem to solve

It is not at all surprising that we get caught up in 'thinking' mode and then propelled like a ball in a pinball machine to acting on these thoughts when we consider the messages that we are bombarded with all day long about how our body *should look,* what jobs we *should have* and what sort of parent, employee, employer, friend or partner, etc. we *should be.*

Along with all this we live in a society that is geared towards a medical-ised view of our bodies and health. If we experience sadness or anxiety, or any uncomfortable physical manifestation of these emotions, we assume that these are a problem and that they need fixing straight away. Our thinking mind pipes up, we start to evaluate our experience, judge it and analyse it, we take ourselves off to the doctor and say, *look, I am anxious, my heart is beating fast,* or *I am sad, I can't get the energy back to get out of my bed, what's wrong with me?* We overanalyse and focus on these experiences as *the problem,* but they are not, they are *the symptom.* It is more to do with the way that we think and focus on these and try to fix and eradicate them, as if they were a problem (and as if that were possible), that is the *real* problem and makes these symptoms even worse.

If it is our attempt to eradicate painful feelings via our endless attempts to think through them, avoid them and solve them and the inherent struggle in this respect that is actually our real problem – then what is the antidote to all this struggling? Well that is the opposite of struggle, letting go of the struggle – letting go of all the over-thinking, problem-solving and trying to push away our 'pain', or in other words *acceptance of what is*, and that's what mindfulness is all about.

What will we do when nothing we do will do?

(as Steven C. Hayes so eloquently says – so we borrowed it!)

> Sometimes I lie awake at night, and I ask, 'Where have I gone wrong?' Then a voice says to me, 'This is going to take more than one night.'
>
> **Charles M. Schulz**

What do we do when we feel busy and overwhelmed? Well, most of us keep *doing*, making plans and new to-do lists, prioritising tasks and doing more – in the hope of getting everything done and making all the stress and 'pain' go away.

What do we tend to do when we feel difficult emotions, discomfort and pain? Well, we usually tend to avoid it, try to get rid of it and keep *busy* to distract ourselves.

A lot of our busyness and associated stress and anxiety to get things done on the surface is a lot more to do with escaping the feelings that are lurking underneath, rather than what we think it's all about – so much to do, things to get done, people to please, success and happiness to get!

With most of the busy people that come to see us for therapy, it is often the case that their busyness is all about trying to get rid of painful and uncomfortable feelings of some type or another. Whether they are busy with work, the kids, socialising, trying to find a partner, or all of the above, when we drill down with them to find out what would happen if they just stopped, let go of any urges to keep all this busyness going, they invariably all admit to feeling scared that if they simply stopped all this *doing* and all that keeps them busy they would feel worthless!

Now, worthlessness is just a word, a term that many of our clients seem to use, along with others like, *not good enough, a failure, rejected, unlovable* – it's just a term that we are now using to describe this painful experience that lurks beneath our busyness; the part of us that we are trying to escape, run away from, that all our busyness distracts us from – you can call it what you want, any term will do! As long as you are honest with yourself and realise that part of you, the underlying feeling that you are trying to run away from and that all your busyness comes from, you can even call it that 'X' if you like! Remember, feelings of worthlessness are very scary to us ALL, we have internalised a prehistoric message from our ancient ancestors that these feelings are connected to our downfall, in other words:

Worthlessness = Death/The End

It is not at all surprising therefore that we would all struggle with these feelings, that we would try our best to avoid, escape or try our hardest to hide them from ourselves or others.

In our modern times, us busy people believe that we need to be busy; if we're not busy getting everything done and attended to then our life will fall apart! We are not idiots and anything we do has a function or some reward otherwise we simply wouldn't bother doing it.

> **"In our modern times, us busy people believe that we need to be busy."**

However, most of us live in a fantasy a lot of the time and believe that if we stopped being so busy, doing and getting everything done, then the world might end and of course that would be tragic! But how often have we stopped to think what would really happen if we just let go and didn't rush around *doing* all the time?

▶ How devastating would it really be?

▶ What really is the very worst thing that would actually happen?

▶ Would our world really come to an almighty sudden crash and traumatic ending?

Well the reality is no, of course it wouldn't! All we are actually trying to avoid is our own feelings, our vulnerability and imperfections. Some of us know this and still fear that once all this is exposed and revealed to ourselves and/or possibly to others – then our world will end, but nothing is the end of the world except the end of the world – these are just feelings and no one will die, no one's world will end simply as a result of you experiencing all this. The feelings that you may be trying to run from are part of you, part of the human experience for all of us – we're all in the same boat here; you can't run from them and you can't hide, so better get used to sitting with them or you'll just get more stressed and busier trying not to! Try to invite all your experience in, it's kinder to yourself when you try to find a way into your life instead of desperately trying to find a way out of it all the time. The very fact that we are terrified of experiencing a part of us is actually telling us what is most important to us, what we want and need more of, which is often a greater sense of safety and security that we can actually give directly to ourselves with more self-directed attention, care, compassion and connectedness (in other words, mindfulness).

So next time you feel rushed off your feet, busier than the busiest bee in town, try the following exercise, which comes in two parts (you may like to use the audio guide to assist with the second part).

▶ First, answer the questions to get to the bottom of what feeling/s lie beneath all *your* busyness.

▶ Keep asking the questions until you get to the feelings that you are trying to avoid within yourself (possibly around feeling failure or rejection or both, or the like).

▶ Then second, just sit with your sense of busyness and see what comes up for you, be aware of, but remember try to resist any urges to run, distract yourself, or get stuff done:

Exercise 7.1: Mindfulness on-the-go

What's underneath my busyness?

Part 1: Drilling down

Ask yourself the following questions:

1 If I DON'T act on this urge right now (to go out, work on this project, check and answer emails, check my Twitter and Facebook messages, call a friend, boss, mother, etc.) what am I really concerned might happen?

2 And what is the problem with that/what might happen then?

3 And what is the problem with that/what might happen then?

4 And what is the problem with that?... For example I will feel 'X' (worthless, failure, rejection, unlovable, etc.).

Part 2: Stop stirring the pond

1 Right, so there it is, your 'X' (e.g. feelings of worthlessness) with all the busyness, stress, anxiety and frustration whirling around it.

2 Now for a few minutes, just sit observing this experience, and any feelings of anxiety, frustration, busyness and stress.

3 Let these feelings come and go as they naturally will. Notice the urges to act on these feelings or any urges to take the feelings away. Notice how the intensity of these feelings and urges change.

4 Notice any thoughts that arise, maybe about how this is not helpful, you have too much to do, there's not enough time in the day for this mindfulness lark! Allow these thoughts to come and go as if they are passing clouds in the sky of your awareness.

5 Now focus in on one of the most intense feelings you have, maybe a feeling of worthlessness or associated fear, anxiety, sadness, general stress or frustration. Locate that feeling in your body; is it in your chest, head, shoulders, heart, legs? If you feel it all over your body then hold your whole body in your awareness.

6 Hold this feeling of pain in your attention, like a caring parent will hold a child, give it your time and attention right now, you don't have to like it, just hold it.

7 Now breathe into and around this feeling. As you breathe out let go of all struggle and tension you may have with this feeling, imagine your out breath carrying this struggle away.

8 Again, breathe into and around this feeling. And as you breathe out, let go of all struggle and tension you may have with this feeling.

9 The feeling may change or it may not, remember the goal is not to change the feeling but to accept it, it's part of you, it makes you human, we all experience it, let it be.

Time to get REAL

Mucking about and struggling with difficult emotions tends to create more of them, not less. We get frustrated that we are still feeling anxious, we are anxious about our anger, we are bored with always being anxious, depressed about always feeling stressed. This is time-consuming and inefficient. This gets in the way of us reaching our targets and goals. This is certainly therefore, the moment to get REAL. This acronym can help remind us of this and what we can do when we meet difficulties, feel overwhelmed and at our wits' end and stands for:

R Recognising (we notice).

E Experiencing (we are open rather than pushing away).

A Analysing (we explore and are curious).

L Letting go (we let go of using an experience to define who we are).

Recognising: Imagine that it is raining, tipping down and you are standing in it. You can think about the rain, plan what to do, how you imagine being later all wet and soggy, create your very own 'it's raining and it's sh*t' story. This is not quite what is meant by recognising. Try instead to notice with your senses. Awaken to the sounds, smells, touch, tastes and look of the rain – remember you don't have to like it just recognise and notice it.

Experiencing: An umbrella may go up, we may dash for shelter or strew our clothes across the ground and dance with wild abandon. This is not important. This is just a moment, just a moment we are experiencing, we can just allow it to be and leave it alone. If we raise our fists to the sky and curse the rain god, or weep further rainy tears for our misfortunes, we have probably missed a window for experiencing and for acceptance (don't worry though, unlike buses, there'll be another chance coming along … oh, right now). No matter how much we rally against reality the rain is very unlikely to stop just because we don't like it and we bet you know really, that it isn't personal! It's not 'just your rotten luck' it 'just is'.

Analysing: Now we see this moment and as we haven't reacted from our usual habitual 'thinking and doing' tendencies, our avoidance tactics, we get to see the situation in a new light. The rain seeping in through our collar, flattening our stylishly coiffured bouffant, why not take a moment to curiously explore planet 'wet'.

Letting go: Now that we have enlivened our senses to this moment, allowed it just to be as it is and had a little sniff around, it could be that it isn't too bad after all, even if it is a bit grim, we can probably bear it. We may even come to the realisation that it is simply rain. By golly! Not a personal vendetta of the storm clouds to get you and ruin your day after all!

This is life, Jim ...

You may like to kid yourself that you are a Vulcan like Spock and are ever so logical. Emotions don't come into the equation of a busy life or making quick rational decisions and your 'feelings' are simply not compatible with good business, performance, success and staying on top of your game. This is a fun idea perhaps, and quite nice for the next Star Trek convention, but it is simply not true. Whoever told you this was possible was misinformed – it's all a trick! You are human (really). You may not like it, sometimes it basically sucks, but there you have it. Now we know all this touchy-feely stuff about emotions and feelings is all a bit fluffy and uncomfortable so, just so you get the point and allow your anxiety about turning into a bare-footed tree-hugger to drift past like a cloud in sky (ahh), here is another nice science bit to help you get the message that emotions are really, honestly, very, very important and yes, you do have them.

You are human (really). You may not like it, sometimes it basically sucks, but there you have it.

As psychologists we recognise that emotional pain is often rooted in early childhood experiences. The human brain is not born fully developed, so early experiences are highly significant in shaping our brain function, neurology and biochemical responses to stress. Think nice, round blob of Play-Doh.

We now understand that cognitions (our thinking minds) are dependent on emotions – as Sue Gerhardt points out: 'Cognitive processes elaborate emotional processes but could not exist without them'. In essence, our higher brain function, such as making sense of our emotions through our thought processes, develops later than our basic 'old brain'. So as tiny babies we can express basic physiological needs through crying, etc. But we are totally dependent on our experiences – such as physical contact, care and nurturing – from an adult to meet those needs and also to then help our brains to develop. Think of making a gentle dent into the Play-Doh with your thumb.

If our needs are not met, or met poorly, we suffer, at the most primal levels this is akin to feeling like we are going to die. This is as dramatic as it sounds because we are absolutely helpless as infants, we also do not have the developed higher levels of cortical (brain) functioning to understand or make sense of the situation. Think fist splatting Play-Doh into a pancake.

This brain functioning does develop but it takes several years, hence children go through differing levels of comprehension – including the egotistical age of two, not believing in the tooth fairy anymore (your parents were liars) and painting your room black as a misunderstood teen. You probably recognise some or all of these stages, but together they make a tower of different coloured blobs and splats of Play-Doh.

So the quality of the relationship between an adult and the child profoundly influences brain structure and biochemistry. If this process lacks sensitivity then our cognitive development is impaired, we don't understand our emotions and we do not experience ways to regulate them, our levels of physiological arousal, associated with emotion are easily either aggravated or suppressed. Splat the whole tower.

The good news is that, even as an adult, we can create new and improved neurological pathways, we can learn to regulate our emotions, we need to work hard to establish these by practising again and again, but this will also get easier and easier to do. Roll the Play-Doh into a cool giant rainbow blob, or any other shape you like.

We can then use REAL (recognising, experiencing, analysing and letting go). We recognise our physiological arousal, we let ourselves experience it and thus do not repeat or reinforce our habitual response, then we analyse it by reflecting mindfully on this response, and we 'let go' through non-attachment and offer ourselves up a nice new neurological pathway. Point being:

Coping with emotions

=

Less stress

=

Better mental and physical health

=

Greater effectiveness and getting ahead in life.

Exercise 7.2: I haven't got time for this practice

Really?

1 **Recognise** any physical sensations happening right now (bum on chair, foot on floor, breath, etc.).

2 Allow yourself just to **experience** these as they are.

3 **Analyse** the experience, perhaps labelling it (discomfort, tension, etc.).

4 **Let it go**. Especially any thoughts of 'dialogue'. Just leave it be, no need to change it or hang on to it.

5 If you want to carry on a bit more, maybe see how another part of your body feels right now and then revisit the original site and go through the steps again.

Mindfulness top tips to-go

OK. So in this chapter you have learned that it is helpful to:

▶ Try to identify and acknowledge your emotions (the good and the bad).

▶ Let all your emotions into your experience.

▶ Stop trying to figure out or get rid of emotions, this will only stress you out more and make you busier and inefficient.

➤

- ▶ Discover what vulnerable feelings lurk beneath and motivate all your busy behaviour.
- ▶ Stop trying to avoid your deeper vulnerabilities and imperfections; you are human after all.
- ▶ Try to find a way into your life, rather than out of it; let all your emotions in.
- ▶ Hold your painful emotions in your awareness, stop struggling with them, breathe into and accept them.
- ▶ Transform your relationship with your emotions by recognising, experiencing, analysing and letting go of them.
- ▶ Practise mindfulness of your physiological arousal (we will be coming back to this a little later).

We are now going to give you some more ideas and helpful tips to manage some specific difficult and challenging emotions – the party poopers.

8

Boredom and distraction

In this chapter we are going to:

- ▶ Discover boredom.
- ▶ Understand what lurks beneath it.
- ▶ Notice how it is a common visitor to our busy lives.
- ▶ Find ways to notice it so we can be more productive in life, rather than distracting ourselves.

For many of us boredom is as much a part of our busy lives as is stress. Sticking to the same routines and schedules day in and day out can become rather mundane and thrill-zapping. Add to this the little time that our busy lives allow for fun and frolics, being so busy can be a real drag most of the time. Boredom is also a well-known phenomenon in mindfulness itself and is particularly … yawn … common in the longer practices, but you may just notice it lingering all day somewhere around about. Sorry? Did you say something? … It usually is a companion to distraction … Oooh, did you see that? … What were we saying? … You know about distraction right? There is just that other thing that you need to do which is a lot more important, and if this chapter would just be a bit more interesting then you might read some more, but right now, all of this waffling on and on and on is just so boooooring! And do you know what else? If you have to sit here and pay attention to any more breaths or sips of coffee or whatever the next crazy thing it might be, you are going to soon find, you might be getting impatient and frustrated, which you would rather avoid so … hmm, did you leave the iron on? Didn't we have to be somewhere else right now?

OK, you're smart, you get this already. But let us explain a bit more here. Boredom and distraction are often like a first layer in emotion, masking over something else. Usually they serve a purpose as strategies for avoiding something, such as even MORE uncomfortable feelings like impatience, fear, sadness or grief. We already know that our instinctual aversion to these emotions helps to maintain any beliefs we hold that tell us these are best left alone, that we might not be able to cope or that if we find such feelings they may go on forever.

> "*Boredom is giving us a helpful clue that we are avoiding something, that we feel uncomfortable.*"

Already boredom is giving us a helpful clue that we are avoiding something, that we feel uncomfortable and we want it to go away (this is the 'recognising' in REAL). Mindfulness can become a fertile ground for boredom as we learn to stay with the urge to avoid (the 'experiencing' in REAL). This can be done by adopting an attitude of curiosity (the 'analysing' in REAL)... oh look, I am bored to tears, how very interesting! Perhaps we can let go, allow our habitual thoughts and urges to 'do something about it' just to pass, to dissolve (the 'letting go' in REAL). But then, back comes our habitual mind, sometimes as quick as a flash – yourthoughtsracingatahundredmilesanhourshiningbrightly-likejewelsthereforthetakingooohpretty! But then still you come back to feeling a little dissatisfied, contacting the boredom, life perhaps feeling a bit like a limp lettuce leaf right now but overthereisalovelynewthinga majigandifIthinkaboutthatIwon'thavetothinkabouthowcrappylifeis! But that too is transient and so we begin to crave something else, some new sensation to take us away from our pain, and each time we do this we push away our life, we reject our true feelings, we reject ourselves. We are probably traipsing down one of those old familiar neural pathways. As soon as we avoid the present moment, here and now, we start to increase a sense of dissatisfaction and urge to get rapidly away from it into doing something (another to-do list perhaps? Or how about reformatting that spreadsheet?). We actually perpetuate our boredom and dissatisfaction with life, ironically we increase our pain, our busyness and layer it over with an illusion (like finding something else to do). But when we do something drastically different, like mindfulness, and get REAL to our emotions we often recognise what we are up to, what we have been avoiding and papering over, and in this case, it is boredom.

Papering over a difficult emotion like boredom with pretty wallpaper is an engaging, busy and full-time activity. It is very like decorating a house that has poor foundations, damp, subsidence and a pest infestation. Instead of noticing the damage, accepting that things are a bit shaky, investigating the problems fully and calling in an objective expert, we spend endless hours worrying that someone might notice something is wrong unless we very cleverly keep busy, propping up the freshly papered walls and setting mouse traps. The truth is also, that when we are busy doing this we fail to also notice that because everyone around us is busy doing the same thing they aren't really seeing what we're up to at all. And there are so many ways to keep up the pretence, just watch the ads on telly – perhaps a new shampoo will be the answer to your woes? No, then try a new car? A great rate of interest on that mortgage? A trip abroad? The possibilities are endless. More distractions, more opportunities to avoid boredom, two for the price of one; more ways to perpetuate your dissatisfaction with life each more promising than the last. It's not your fault, life is full of fascinating ideas, objects and sensations – perhaps we have just forgotten that *we* too are one of those – right here, right now. When did we turn into the interior decorator, the builder and the pest-controller? Whose house is this anyway? How about pulling back that paper and finding the door and walking on out into the fresh air? Go on!

"Life is full of fascinating ideas, objects and sensations – perhaps we have just forgotten that we too are one of those. "

Exercise 8.1: Mindfulness reflection moment

Boredom test (N.B.: there are some clues in BOLD)

R: Recognising:

▶ What tells you you are bored?

– (Chose one): The dog; Waiting; The news; The clock; Silence; **YOU**

▶ What distracts you from boredom?

– (Chose any): Food; TV; Twitter; Facebook; Talking; Drink; Texting; Sex; Magazines; Exercise; Work; Radio; DIY; Drugs; Drawing; Smoking; Cleaning; Worrying; Holidays; Gambling; Daydreaming; Driving fast; Bird-watching; Clubbing; Plate-spinning; Inventing; Sleeping; **YOU**

▶ How bored are you now?

– Rate from: 0% (manically consumed with enthusiasm for myself and all) – 100% (I am about to eat my own head from boredom).

E: Experiencing:

▶ How can you open up to this experience? (Pick what helps.)

– Reminding myself of the Zen saying: 'If you understand, things are just as they are. If you do not understand, things are still just as they are.'

– Repeating 'just this one breath, just this one moment'.

– Try holding the thought/feeling/sensation with gentleness.

- Imagining myself as a mountain, solid whatever the weather.
- Something else.

▶ How much am I able to be present with this right now?
- (Chose one): Not able/a wee bit/sort of/willing and able/oh so Zen baby.

▶ What can I tell myself about this experience? (Pick one.)
- I can't do it.
- I'm failing.
- I'm too bored or distracted right now.
- I'm stuck.
- **WOW, HOW INTERESTING, I'M BORED.**

A: Analysing

▶ When mindfully exploring this emotion it is possible to develop … (Pick one.)
- A rash.
- Master plans for world domination.
- A novel titled *Memoirs of a Bore*.
- All of the above.
- **AWARENESS AND INSIGHT.**

▶ Taking a stance of curiosity cultivates (pick all):
- Interest.
- Enthusiasm.
- Validation of ourselves.
- Awareness.
- Honesty.
- Courage.
- Willingness.

▶ Helpful imagery might include imagining myself as (pick all – yes we mean it … except the last one):
- A scientist.
- An explorer.
- A martian.
- A monkey.
- Napoleon.

L: Letting go:

▶ Letting go of boredom is (pick one):

- Pushing it away.
- Pretending it is not there and going la la la la la la
- Beating myself up for feeling like this … again!
- Diving into stories of my miserable, dull little life.
- Finding something else to do like sky-diving, or crochet, or, or …
- A dangerous path towards coldness, detachment and lack of care.
- **GENTLY LETTING GO OF A HABIT AND SIMPLY WATCHING IT.**

▶ What might I be when I'm not bored? (Pick any, plus the last one.)

- Frustrated.
- Disappointed.
- Afraid.
- Interesting.
- Passionate.
- Crazy.
- Liberated.
- I don't know.
- **A LITTLE MORE ALIVE TO NOW.**

▶ Letting go can be aided by (chose any):

- Noticing, watching and observing my thoughts, emotions, sensations, behaviours and habits.
- Mentally stepping back.
- Being open to other possibilities.
- Just letting go.
- I don't know yet! That's why I'm reading this book you twit.

Maybe when you have one of 'those meetings' at work, or spend time with an ageing relative, are in a long queue or at a parents' evening this would be an extra good moment to maximise meeting your pal boredom. Of course boredom pounces (or limps) upon us many times in our lives, so just use the following techniques during your usual day.

Exercise 8.2: Mindfulness on-the-go

Bored meeting

Try it:

1 Notice how you know you feel bored. Perhaps if there is something specially 'bored' about your posture, your facial expression, your breathing or thoughts.

2 Notice this and return your attention to it over and over.

3 Breathe, slump, grimace or whatever else *with* your boredom.

4 Be aware of the breath rising and falling throughout this moment.

5 Maybe the boredom is changing, all by itself, or maybe it is sticking around right now.

6 Encourage yourself to examine this moment. Perhaps even imagining you are new to boredom and looking at it afresh, like a martian or monkey with an irrepressible curiosity; picking stuff up and sniffing it. Engage with it, be alive to your boredom.

7 If it is difficult, let it go. It is only an experience, only sensations, only a moment.

8 Each time you let go of your struggle with this emotion you are letting go of a lifetime's habitual way of thinking and responding to it – just one breath at a time.

Mindfulness top tips to-go

In this chapter you have learned that it is helpful to:

▶ Take a closer look at your boredom.

▶ Notice that boredom and distraction often tell us that we are avoiding something, some uncomfortable feeling that we'd like to get rid of.

▶ Understand boredom in the context of your busy life.

▶ Think about how you can respond to boredom mindfully.

▶ Practise a mindfulness exercise around boredom.

Sleepiness, fantasising and physical discomfort

We are now going to turn your attention towards a few other niggles that show up throughout our busyness and often get in the way of being more mindful. In this chapter you will:

▶ Understand ways of coping with sleeplessness (insomnia), sleepiness and lethargy.

▶ Discover how we tend to try to escape our busy realities via fantasy and daydreaming.

▶ Learn how restlessness and sleepiness are often ways of trying to avoid uncomfortable emotions.

▶ Learn how you can better cope with common physical aches and pain.

These are wonderful party poopers! They often arrive with boredom … sneaking in when the door is still open. Now, of course we need to clarify that there is absolutely nothing wrong with these party guests from time to time. Be honest, come on, haven't you ever sat so long your legs get stiff, without even noticing, until you stand up like something from *Dawn of the Dead*? Or fallen asleep during your dinner/meetings about tax/culturally important arty film? Or thought about that really sexy person on the tube just a little longer than absolutely necessary and missed your stop? No? Perhaps that's just us then … But, still, we're sure you'll each recognise these when they occur, and often we actually do need some more sleep, or to move position, it is a gesture of our self-care and kindness to respond appropriately to these needs as they arise rather than wilfully staying with them. However, it may be that you discover another form of these innocuous looking little friends; the occasions when they seem to turn up *all* the time (weddings, birthdays and bar mitzvahs). In a similar way to boredom, sleepiness, fantasising and physical discomfort (or restlessness) can actually be habitual and are also usually forms of avoidance (of painful feelings). So, yes, clever clogs, we know sleepiness, fantasising and physical discomfort are not *really* emotions and we are just taking a little artistic licence squeezing them in here. However, when we greet them, we see another layer of our habitual thinking mind, stalking about and putting us off the trail to our emotions, take some notice and they will show you what treasures they are hiding (the ones you have been avoiding). We will now look a little more closely at each in turn.

> ❝Sleepiness, fantasising and physical discomfort can actually be habitual and are also usually forms of avoidance.❞

Sleepiness

This probably takes the least explanation. Normally, if you feel tired our highly psychologically insightful recommendation would be … to sleep. This is sometimes easier said than done when you are really busy and your mind is racing and you are basically a tad frenetic. Nevertheless, if you are even able to notice, then the good news is, you are at least aware of your need for more rest. And the even better news is that we can get a lot of rest just by being in awareness (even more than when running from the boogieman when we're fast asleep).

If a sense of tiredness arises regularly, especially during times when you are attempting to focus your attention on the present moment, and an important task at hand, then it could also be a snuggly, warm blanket-shaped sign of something uncomfortable, an unpleasant emotion you may be avoiding. Poor sleep patterns are symptoms of a lot of mental health problems, such as depression, so it is great to notice, and now, rather than avoiding sleep issues. And we are going to help you find new ways of taking care of this difficulty.

Sometimes we can feel tired when we are getting ill, and mindful attention can help us chose an appropriate early intervention which may prevent greater suffering, either physically or mentally (and probably both). You might even find yourself in the habit of wilfully forcing your way through these feelings, trying to push on regardless, or fuel yourself through the day with caffeine or drugs, just to make it to work, or get through a meeting or even just to get up at all. We have here an alternative suggestion, and the good news is – you can stay in bed!

Try this next mindfulness practice as soon as you can. Here are some helpful pointers:

- For the purposes of this practice it makes no difference if you fall asleep or not.
- If you do have to be somewhere, it might be useful to decide how long you want to practise before beginning and set an alarm or have someone gently wake you if you do fall asleep.
- Remember to use the principles of REAL (recognising, experiencing, analysing and letting go) when you are noticing your sleepiness and sleeplessness.
- It may be that as you practise this you become aware of how punitive you usually are to pushing away your tiredness and refusing to sleep – a basic physical need.

You may like to use the audio guide to assist you in this practice.

Right, so let's get snug ...

Exercise 9.1: I haven't got time for this practice

Duvet-diving mindfulness

This takes about 60 seconds – or all day if you want:

1 Get yourself comfy and allow yourself to settle into this moment, in your bed.

2 Notice the position of your body, just as it is.

3 Become aware of the contact of the duvet with your body.

4 Become aware of the sensations where your body makes contact with the soft bouncy mattress.

5 Observe any warmth, softness and cosiness around you.

6 Observe any restlessness or fidgeting in your body.

7 Keep returning to these sensations, developing an interest and curiosity in them.

8 Be aware of thoughts arising, perhaps urges to fall asleep or get up, try staying just as you are, and watch those thoughts and urges drifting around.

9 Bring your focus of attention to now, softly held in your duvet.

10 There you are, in your bed, aware of postures, all sensations, emotions, thoughts.

11 Just for this moment, there is nothing else to do.

Noticing your posture can also be very helpful in alleviating habitual tiredness throughout the day, so be sure that you allow your physical body to support your intention to be alert (when you want to be) by sitting openly – try sitting on the edge of a chair or standing up and keep your eyes open if you want to stay focused throughout the day! (It is very hard to sleep with your eyes open despite the rumours about Bruce Lee.)

You may notice, that as you begin to develop curiosity around your sleepiness or sleeplessness, you find something else, that perhaps habitual sleepiness or sleeplessness has previously masked, is revealed. You may then need to move on to the relevant chapter and exercise in this book to help you to investigate this further. It may well be the use of mindfulness and the good attention you have given to yourself, that you are able to break an unhelpful relationship with sleepiness or sleeplessness and begin to wake up to your life, right now.

Fantasising

It may seem to you, like it does to us, that *if only* things would get a little less hectic, slow down and back away, then life would be so much easier, and of course mindfulness would surely be a doddle. Sometimes we may find ourselves being a little indulgent in our imaginings.

The tropical beach, for instance is a particular favourite:

> A holiday at an island in Indonesia ... there was a lovely beach hut just a moment's white-sanded stroll from the sea, with a tropical reef full of iridescent fish just metres from the shore. There was no one else there ... it was amazingly cheap and there were a whole five weeks promised ahead ... Ahh bliss!

(Of course memory has down-graded the mosquitoes, sun burn and lack of electricity.)

Those were the kinds of times we might imagine, or recall (selectively) when we were or could be *really happy and calm* and really, really sorted, so that we could cope with anything. Or maybe if we write this book *really, really* well and it is fun, engaging and life-changing we will be admired and loved by all – move over Jerry Springer. Or a different partner, perhaps 'the one that got away', surely we would not argue with them, they would really 'get' us and we would be 10lbs slimmer, as we run, laughing, hand-in-hand towards the sunset on that Indonesian beach? Maybe you dream of fame, fortune, adventure, love or escape to peaceful solitude?

Perhaps, like all of us, you think that if life was just different in some ways (less busy and hectic, smaller nose, bigger house, better sex, promotion, less rain, stronger body, honest politicians, etc.) *then* we could be OK, we could at least find our way, maybe sustain it and actually *enjoy* life a bit. Fantasy, in particular, can look innocent enough, and often is, however, it can also be the poisoned chalice that taints our world by promising 'real happiness' and leaving us dissatisfied with our lot. When we begin to crave past experiences, alternative realities or a perfect future we are inadvertently rejecting the present and ourselves along with it. By looking for something else, something a bit better, more of a 'good' time, we are also saying 'this is not good enough'. That might even be true sometimes, and then we have acceptance, but change the emotional tone to one of perpetual dissatisfaction and we see the repetitiveness, the undermining of anything pleasant or 'positive' anyway, we just want more.

> ❝When we begin to crave past experiences, alternative realities or a perfect future we are inadvertently rejecting the present and ourselves along with it. ❞

Imagine going on a date, being dressed in your glad-rags and sitting down for some scintillating conversation over a miniature plate of expensive morsels. Your date is not looking at you, not talking to you and not even picking at the food. Instead they are constantly looking over your shoulder, scanning the room, checking their phone, fidgeting and no matter what you do, your date just is not interested. This is you. When you fantasise constantly about something better, this is what you are doing to yourself, over and over. Just a bit depressing, isn't it? Not only that, but this can get harmful too, the fantasy can be inflated further through gambling, dieting, compulsive behaviours, promiscuity, drug-taking or just about any other activity when done to excess. So, we've exploded the myth of 'having a good time', because, when it gets like this it is actually 'avoiding a bad time'. When we notice this we are undoing all that avoidance, we are seeing life as it is. We see, hopefully with a little grace, that we are sat right in the poo, and guess what? That person over there laughing just a bit too loud is probably up to their eyeballs in it too. So, nice to know we are not alone. We'll pick up on this again in the next part of the book, but this recognition, this ability to experience life in all its colours can actually also enliven us to the shared experiences of others, it very naturally allows in a sense of companionship, empathy, kindness and compassion.

Try this following **Mindfulness on-the-go** exercise as often as you can as you bustle about your busy existence and notice that you might be engaged in unhelpful habits such as fantasising or daydreaming. It's a great and very quick way to help you wake up and feel alive and make contact with your life, your rich, present moment experience, whatever that may be.

Exercise 9.2: Mindfulness on-the-go

Sense-sational

▶ Stop, right now, whatever you are doing (maybe reading this book), wherever you are.

▶ Look up and around you.

▶ Take a breath.

▶ Invite all of yourself in.

▶ Awaken from the dream.

▶ **Notice the colours, hear the sounds, smell the scents, touch the textures and savour the taste of your life right now.** *This is it.*

Repeat the above whenever you become aware of fantasising or acting in unhelpful fantasy-prompted behaviours. See if you notice the realisation occurring that even if you have a strong desire to escape reality, you do not *need* to act on this. You can arrive at this moment here and now and allow the sense of freedom and relief to arise and rush into this moment, which comes along with letting go.

Physical discomfort

Knee-jerk reactions

Being busy most of the time leads to high levels of adrenalin rushing around our bodies, this is just the case even if we are busy in our minds and not that physically active from day-to-day. Our bodies can tell us quite a lot about how busy and stressed we are in any given moment. It is often the case that for many of us busy people that it is not until we notice our heart beating fast, a shortness of breath, a headache, feeling dizzy, shaky, lethargic or that we pull a muscle or the like – or a combination of the above – that we even realise that we have been rushing around on autopilot, stressed out, for far too long.

> *"Being busy most of the time leads to high levels of adrenalin rushing around our bodies."*

Mindfulness practice invites us to not only notice and become aware of our feelings, thoughts and behaviours but also of our bodies and the varied sensations that we may come to experience in them. Without this awareness we may simply be increasing our stress levels and overall sense of busyness day-to-day without even knowing it. Just as our thoughts and feelings interact with one another, our bodies and emotions do the same.

There is a feedback loop between our bodies and our emotional experience, which can lead to an overall busier and more stressful experience in life. If you smile you'll feel instantly happier (go on try it now, you know you want to). If you frown you could feel sadder or more stressed.

Similarly if you walk fast with your head down and protruding forward you will no doubt feel busier and more stressed. It is important to observe and notice our bodies in this way. We can wake up to how they are in any given moment, what they are telling us, what messages they are sending to our emotions and could then alleviate a lot of our emotional discomfort by making some simple bodily adjustments.

When we experience some physical aches or pains, such as tightness in our chest, our heart beating fast or tension in our shoulders we often try to get rid of it, stretching and contracting that body part in an attempt to ease the physical discomfort. Sometimes such efforts can simply make it worse. It is important to notice how we are responding to our physical sensations as much as it is to the emotions and thoughts that come and go in our experience. If we don't we run the risk of feeling more stressed out and causing ourselves more physical pain. When you notice physical discomfort instead of struggling with it try to bring more mindful attention to the experience, holding that discomfort with some more kindness – you might like to try getting REAL or some of the other exercises in Chapter 7 to remind you how to do this.

Exercise 9.3: Mindfulness reflection moment

Body sculpting

Think about how your body is, what posture it takes when you are at your most stressed and busy. The chances are that you will notice it's bent over, shoulders clenched, head down, closed, tight and tensed up, maybe hands up on your forehead and so on.

▶ Take a moment to imagine that posture now or even better (if you are willing, go on, no one's looking) try getting into this stressed out, busy posture now to remind yourself what it's like.

Now, how about when you're feeling less pressured, more relaxed and with an overall sense of well-being (if you can remember such a time), how's your body and posture then?

▶ Take a moment to think about that now or again even try getting into this more relaxed posture right now.

What did you notice? The chances are that your head is held high, chin is up, shoulders back and gently dropped at your sides, chances are that your body is in a more overall open position.

These two quite oppositional postures will not only be reflective of your mood but will also go on to impact on your mood in the same way – it's circular. The questions to ask yourself are:

▶ What does it really take to get from the first posture to the second described?

▶ Does the world need to be any different, do you have to be less busy, have less demanding and annoying people around you?

Well no, nothing more than noticing and gentle realigning.

Exercise 9.4: Mindfulness on-the-go

Body realignment

So throughout your busy days:

▶ Bring more awareness to your body, its posture and your habitual urges to respond to unpleasant body sensations.

▶ Make a purposeful effort to notice when your shoulders are up around your ears and gently drop them, realign your posture to an upright and relaxed pose rather than it being bent over and all tensed up no matter how busy or stressed you feel.

▶ Instead of instinctively acting on a knee-jerk reaction to push or pull unwanted sensations away, notice them, let go of any urges to struggle with them, get REAL to them or move gently if you choose to – or you may find you do yourself a mischief!

We have figured out through extensive Googling on your behalf that the average red light lasts for between 30 and 60 seconds. Next time you are in your car or walking to work and you come across a red light try this next on-the-go exercise. You may even try this as you stand waiting for the train doors to open at your stop. Try it as often as you like to really start to wake up to your body and its natural habits and impulsive knee-jerk reactions.

Exercise 9.5: Mindfulness on-the-go

In the red: how to stop at a traffic light (or alight from a train carriage)

1 Stop.

2 How's your body right now?

3 Do you notice your feet itching to rev the peddle, step in front of the pizza delivery bike whizzing past or squeeze through the slit between the train doors?

4 Can you feel any sensations in your neck or shoulders like tension, tightness or even an absence of these?

5 What is your face doing? Is it scowling, frowning or grinning? Does it feel all hard or soft like a fuzzy peach?

6 What happens when the light changes (doors open)? What does your body do?

7 See if you can move through the green light (or train doors) and carry your mindfulness along with you.

A pain in the a*se

Everyone who sits still for a period of time (like with your nose pressed up against a computer screen at your desk all day long) will inevitably experience a level of discomfort, especially if you are not used to it. During the day, most of us find that we respond to discomfort with those 'knee-jerk reactions' we just mentioned.

When we make adjustments mindfully, and come to a place of rest and stillness, then we see the merit in movement and are acting towards self-care. Awareness of this can be very beneficial. Lack of awareness can leave us living with discomfort we might not be responding to in the most effective way; we can be prone to ignoring our discomfort, disowning it, being frustrated, dismissive and irritated with it. *The pain in my a*se, is so annoying, it is a real pain in the a*se, and so are you! And the world around you!*

These responses to physical representations of discomfort are absolutely the same as we have towards mental and emotional discomfort. Awareness and acceptance can lead to acknowledgements and the need for change as an expression of self-care (just like getting an extra cushion for our a*se to sit on, drinking when thirsty, or perhaps a realisation that you need to resolve a disagreement with someone). Alternatively, awareness of habitual tendencies of fidgeting, ignoring the problem and/ or 'getting on with it' may be noticed as unhelpful.

There are basically four types of experiences with our physical discomfort:

1 Fleeting adjustments to posture or calls of nature (needing the loo, being cold, hungry, tired, etc.).
2 Fidgeting or restlessness.
3 Short-term pain or discomfort.
4 Long-term pain or illness.

Mindfulness can help us to develop a different relationship with *all* of these.

Fleeting adjustments to posture or calls of nature

Hopefully, our body and mind are well enough attuned to respond well to our basic physical needs or the 'calls of nature'. The feedback loop between physical necessities and our emotional response is often very clear here. Just like, for instance, how it can be easier to get angry if we are too hot (think of expressions such as 'hot-headed', 'needing to cool down', 'fiery tempered', etc.). But even these can be disrupted at times and mindfulness is useful in reminding us to check in with our bodies. Try the next exercise as often as you can.

Exercise 9.6: Mindfulness on-the-go

Check me out

1 Whatever activity you are engaged with at the moment, take a pause.

2 With mindful attention scan your body quickly paying attention to:

- Physical tension or comfort.
- Hunger.
- Thirst.
- Temperature.
- The need to go to the loo.
- Tiredness.

3 Just check yourself out, be aware that you have some choice over how you respond – are you reacting automatically? What stories might you be prone to telling? What else have you become aware of?

4 Decide what is the most helpful, supportive and/or appropriate way to respond to yourself.

Fidgeting or restlessness

Persistent fidgeting is often habitual. It is a clear indication that our mind is also restless and distracted and uneasy, accompanied by a sense of pervading dissatisfaction, which is usually ignored. Investigation and exploration of this are very helpful, watch your mind, notice the stories. Engage with your fidgeting as fully as you can. What is the fidgeting telling you? (You may well need to take a look at other sections of this chapter now.)

Short-term pain or discomfort

Short-term pain, discomfort or even illness, although unpleasant, are often tolerated, but have a sense of transience, so unless recurrent, are not as distressing as long-term illness because we usually *relate* to them differently. We can be dismissive and stoic, 'carrying on', especially when we have so much to get done, knowing we will probably get over it soon (although this can be very damaging if we do this too much), we can use over-the-counter medications, do some simple stretching or other ways to take care of ourselves, and sometimes this is sufficient to 'make it go away'. The desire to take away pain is a natural and quite instinctive approach, but we often don't even notice that we're doing it! Our bodies have a helpful way of continuing to niggle at discomfort that needs more attention, even when we might be ignoring it.

A very itchy mosquito bite, calling to you to please, please give it a scratch, for example, or an injury reminding you not to put too much weight on that part of your body, or perhaps a persistent cough. With even the most paltry amount of mindfulness we usually learn what to do pretty quickly, often quite reactively – 'surf' the urge to scratch, keep weight off an injury, get out of the cloud of toxic smoke. However, what if the discomfort keeps on going, the bite doesn't stop itching, the injury doesn't heal, the cough comes back? Then we can find ourselves beginning to build stories to go with the discomfort: the bite becomes a tropical disease, the injury a permanent disability, the cough cancer – oh my, I will never be able get everything done in time now and will just get busier and busier. These stories may or may not be true. They are usually catastrophic, dramatic and unbearable and we, again, instinctively want to get away from them and our pain as quickly as possible. We create *suffering* through our habitual responses to pain or discomfort, when we have pain AND suffering life can feel really appalling.

> ❝ *We create* suffering *through our habitual responses to pain or discomfort.* ❞

This can even become cyclical: pain arises, we push it away, it arises again, we tell ourselves a 'danger story', now we experience mental suffering *and* physical pain, we push it away, pain arises, the story-telling becomes more embellished, we suffer more, we attach to our stories emotionally and they feel true, this is verified to us through the experience of physical pain, the pain becomes more threatening, our body becomes more tense, further pain arises, etc. In fact, it is entirely possible to have physical pain which is *totally* stress-related. Guess what? Mindfulness simply requires attention to the pain and discomfort, to attend to our habitual way of responding. No need to push it away, no need to attach to our stories, just to notice. The pain may or may not disappear, but our suffering can. When we are clear from suffering we may also find ourselves able to relate differently to our pain once we've noticed just exactly what we are dealing with.

Long-term pain or illness

The biggy here, of course is long-term health related issues, which can feel unbearable. But *this too* can be assisted with mindfulness. Unlike our (sometimes) helpful aversion to minor discomfort or pain, which can involve a simple act such as taking medicine or shifting position to functionally aid our bodies; long-term or chronic pain is made extremely difficult to live with when we are so averse to it. Ignoring, distracting or temporarily suppressing pain or discomfort, when it is chronic, doesn't work. With chronic pain, the key is to accept and then to explore and investigate our relationship, to be open to our natural attachment to suffering (*really?* Yes!) and to cultivate compassion (see more on this in Part 4). Mindfulness is not about accepting pain in order to endure, suffer and be wilful. With mindfulness, such as with the following body scan practice, you learn about how you are relating to your pain, you can find openness to now, to be in just one moment at a time, to learn ways to live, just as you are.

> *Ignoring, distracting or temporarily suppressing pain or discomfort, when it is chronic, doesn't work.*

Exercise 9.7: I haven't got time for this practice

Body scanning

Wherever you are, whatever you are engaged with – be it on the train, preparing a report for work, getting the kids ready for a bath, writing an email or checking your smartphone, take three minutes to tune into your body. You may like to use the audio recording to assist you with this practice.

1 Tune into any bodily sensations that you can notice as you continue with your task.

2 Acknowledge and label them like a curious scientist might – 'there is a tightness in my chest' or 'there is an ache in my head'.

3 If your mind comes in to judge this, try to acknowledge your thoughts and return to just noticing and observing the sensation.

4 Finally, notice your posture and stance, scanning your body from head to toe, observing the body in its entirety, whatever you may be doing.

If you find you are having difficulty knowing how to use mindfulness with the kind of pain or physical discomfort you are experiencing you might like to use the flowchart at the end of this chapter to help you.

Mindfulness top tips to-go

In this chapter you have learned that it is helpful to:

▶ Recognise the different guises in which certain kinds of avoidance or distraction from our difficult emotions can appear.

▶ See that often sleepiness, sleeplessness, restlessness, fantasising and physical discomfort are critical factors in reducing our efficiency and concentration.

▶ Notice when you are either ignoring or indulging in these as a way of escaping from other difficult emotions.

▶ Practise mindfulness and awareness around these experiences to alleviate unhelpful patterns and habits.

▶ Pay attention to your sleepiness, sleeplessness, fantasising or physical pain in helpful ways and without inadvertently making them worse.

▶ Free up time and energy and improve your efficiency, concentration and productivity by responding mindfully to sleepiness, sleeplessness, fantasising and physical pain or discomfort.

▶ Fantasise less about alternative perfect realties as in doing so you are rejecting the present and yourself along with it.

▶ Notice your body and all its knee-jerk impulsive reactions as there is a feedback loop between your body and your emotions.

▶ Realign your posture to an open and relaxed pose; it will help you to feel less stressed and busy.

▶ Bring awareness to your physical discomfort and act with mindfulness and self-care.

▶ Bring awareness to your experience of pain, to your relationship with pain, let go of your pain habits to lessen your experience of physical pain.

Exercise 9.8: Mindfulness reflection moment

What kind of a pain are you?

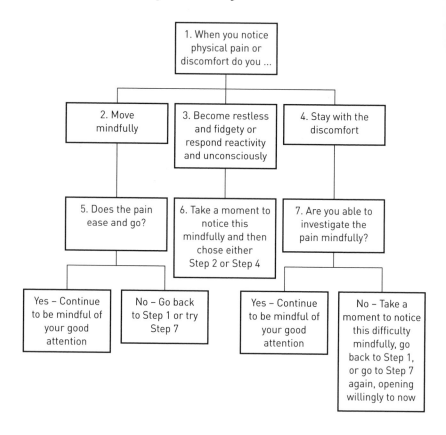

10

Anger, frustration and impatience

Get out the way! Stand back! Cue A-Team music ... get ready for the muscle-bound, modern-day warriors, in they storm, self- righteous and frowning, ready to right wrongs everywhere with their own unique brand of justice. They action-roll away from the exploding warehouse, machine gun firing off rounds, blasting stress and weakness. Now things are really hotting up!

In this chapter we are going to help you to:

▶ Find ways of recognising your anger.

▶ Understand exactly what your anger, frustration or impatience is all about.

▶ Understand how avoiding or getting caught up in anger is often not effective to getting things done and creating the reality you want.

▶ Learn how to manage mindfully when conflict arises in your busy life.

Anger can feel really powerful, we can point the gun at anyone or any-thing that gets in our way and blast it off the face of the earth. Then we never need look at it again. If we are not in a position to act on our anger, we may choose to brood and plot our cold revenge. This can quite possibly lead us towards our old friend 'fantasising', and as we know, this means that we are trying to reject reality and therefore trying to fight it off. Whenever we fight reality, we lose every time. It is time-consuming and a waste of precious time. If your strategy so far has been to come up fighting bigger and stronger, then maybe take a good look at that, because our guess is that it isn't working too well.

Frustration can occur when our anger is suppressed, remains unexpressed or is thwarted, and impatience is a form of anger 'leaking'. These manifestations of anger, may not be quite so 'red hot', but they are often snarling like a couple of guard dogs appearing outwardly as: sarcasm, bitterness, nagging, malicious gossip, complaining, sabotage, playing tricks, derision, insincerity and agitation. You may even notice this very form of anger plastered across your face on a regular basis, doing its bit for Botox, and creating another one of those body–emotion feedback loops we discussed in Chapter 9.

If you do notice that your face often tells a thousand angry stories, then have a go at the next exercise and watch the Botox bills reduce in no time.

Exercise 10.1: Mindfulness reflection moment

Deep impact

If you were to scowl all day long, the chances are that you would feel more stressed and frustrated as a result:

▷ Try it right now.
▷ Scrunch up, wrinkle and contract your brow and notice how you feel emotionally as a result, in this very moment …

How did you go? Did you feel instantly more p'd off? The chances are you did. Similarly, if you tense your stomach muscles or clench your jaw you may feel more agitated and stressed. Go on, give it a go now, gently!

So make a purposeful effort to check in with your angry expression and angry bodily tension, as often as you can and you may find that you are able to lessen your anger by some simple body awareness and realignment (as you have already tried in Exercise 9.4 in the last chapter).

Along with hating the world, anger can also manifest itself inwards towards yourself in the form of a powerful internal self-critic who is constantly belittling you. In fact usually both are occurring. The important thing to remember is that anger is *always* defensive.

So, this big tough nut of an emotion with his/her battle scars and rabid guard dogs has actually got a secret to hide. This secret, like Superman's

Kryptonite, is his/her ultimate vulnerability and 'weakness' and therefore it is necessary to defend, hide and dodge the truth of its existence with all possible power. Anger really is hard. When life is not going our way, when the kids won't shut it, the boyfriend has left the loo seat up *again*, the car won't start, we spilt coffee on our laptop, the train is delayed, we get *another* parking ticket, the boss is having a go, it's raining ... well, life can feel a bit sh*te. Guess what? Our bet is that anger is on its way and it's trying (probably not very well) to make it all go away.

Just to complicate things further and make this difficult emotion even trickier – often we don't even want it! This big bruiser is a bit embarrassing, too loud and unsophisticated; we want it to go away. We might try to pretend it isn't there or just start complaining that feeling anger at all is wrong, unfair and unjust. There is often a sense of urgency to 'make' things we believe are responsible for this anger different, right now! We might notice that our thoughts, speech and actions can be very exaggerated as we attempt to assert our will and we may just see a little in common with a tantruming two-year-old.

If you don't recall these days or do not have access to a handy two-year-old of your own, then pop down to the local supermarket. Stop in an aisle and listen. Often you will hear a screaming sound, somewhat at odds with the music being piped out. Follow the screams and observe – it is quite a treat. Please remember to smile sympathetically at the accompanying adult(s). This little being rolling across the filthy floor, with a contraband packet of biscuits in his or her small sweaty hands, wailing with wild and passionate abandon is the most beautiful possible example of 'thwarted will' or anger. This is us too. We may often appear a little more self-contained (although not always), but the sentiment is the same. As an egotistical two-year-old, it is very normal to think that we are the centre of the universe and it *should* bend to our will, it is also very important to tantrum ... then to be held kindly and be told 'no, little one, it's not like that right now, it's like this, and I know that is hard for you' so that we can grow up psychologically as well as physically. But since this hasn't happened brilliantly for many of us we get a bit stuck at around two years old sometimes (not so tough now, eh?). When we react to our anger by using exaggerated thoughts, speech or action we usually don't help ourselves or others. It is like shouting at that tantruming two-year-old – 'shut up!' (if you've ever tried this you know how hopeless it is, how miserable you end up feeling and how indifferent/scared/more angry your two-year-old becomes). As an adult we have slightly varied our repertoire, but we can spot some very obvious clues if we just tune in a bit with mindfulness. We can see that we often treat anger with louder anger, placation or by ignoring it. Let us turn now, to looking specifically at our speech:

Exercise 10.2: Mindfulness reflection moment

Lippy lingo

When we are angry we tend to use absolutes, which are specific words or phrases that we use to qualify and modify our statements. These words are the adverbs that are all-encompassing. Think back to a time when you, or someone you know, became angry. See from the list below which of these phrases or words you can recall:

▶ You/they/it/she/he always …
▶ You/it/she/he/they never …
▶ Every time
▶ I've told you/him/her/them/it a million times …
▶ Only ever
▶ Impossible
▶ Constantly
▶ All the time
▶ Nobody
▶ Everybody
▶ Every time
▶ Forever
▶ None
▶ Nothing

Here are some examples: You are *always* nagging. You *never* shut up. *Every time* I see you. *I've told you a million times* that I'll get round to it. It *only ever* seems to be like this these days and it is getting *impossible*. You are *constantly* getting at me, *all the bloody time*. *Nobody* else treats me like this, *everybody* else knows I can do it. Really, *every time* I see you, *every time*! You are just *forever* hassling! I want *none* of it! Get it? *N-o-t-h-i-n-g*!

We could even add in a few of our own personal favourite angry catch-phrases: You can't be as busy as me, it's impossible, How dare you! Outside now! I can't stand it! It's over! I've had enough! I can't take any more of this! You never listen to me, it's always about you!

Now watch an episode of Jeremy Kyle or *EastEnders* and be vigilant for these kinds of phrases, add to the lists, and be mindful of what the words do for you, think about how you make statements using these words or phrases, how often you use them when you are arguing and how often you end up debating these words instead of focusing on the real problem.

The real reason for ranting

The intent behind these angry words is to make our viewpoint seem stronger and also to make the other person, people or situation look worse. When we make our statements so universal and absolute, what we are we really fighting for is to somehow put our needs and feelings first – we are actually craving and arguing for acknowledgement.

The use of these words usually serves to undermine us and our point gets lost, which is why anger can be so frustrating, and annoying and we don't seem to get *anywhere, ever*. Although we may want to hurt another with our words (be honest now) or ensure that others look worse than us, we often can feel guilty and upset for the pain that our words seem to have caused a loved one or colleague. Mindfulness will give you a moment of clarity, to understand that what you say might really hurt someone you care for or that it is just really plain unhelpful if you want to get ahead with some task.

There are very few things in life really that never deviate or have any exceptions. We guess that your loved ones or the situation that has given rise to this anger does deviate from the behaviour you hate, at least some of the time. By telling someone that, 'You *always* treat me that way', they (and you too) are then in a kind of trap, which can also give rise to anger as they defend themselves – leading to further discord. An absolute statement or phrase also gives them something else to argue about (the truth of your statement) other than what you are really upset about. This leaves you even further from discussing the actual problem. See? Frustrating! So, what is the alternative?

Take care of your anger

This is THE MOST IMPORTANT bit. There are loads of techniques for calming down: count to ten kind-of-thing, waving flowers at soldiers and plastering a smile over the angry cracks. But none of these is going to mean squat if you haven't noticed how vulnerable you are. Your two-year-old really needs your attention when you are angry. Thich Nhat Hanh writes:

> You have to be like a mother listening for the cries of her baby. If a mother is working in the kitchen and hears her baby crying, she puts down whatever she is doing, and goes to comfort her baby. She may be making a very good soup; the soup is important, but it's much less important than the suffering of her baby. She has to put down the soup, and go to the baby's room. Her appearance in the room is like sunshine because the mother is full of warmth, concern and tenderness. The first thing she does is pick up the baby and embrace him tenderly. When the mother embraces her baby, her energy penetrates him and soothes him. This is exactly what you have to learn to do when anger begins to surface. You have to abandon everything that you are doing, because your most important task is to go back to yourself and take care of your baby, your anger. Nothing is more urgent than taking good care of your baby.
>
> **Anger, p32**

Mindful speech

Step 1: To yourself try

R **Recognising**: 'I notice anger arising' or 'Hello my little two-year-old' or 'Anger'.

E **Experiencing**: 'I am suffering' or 'This is hard' or 'Just this one moment' and 'I'm here to take care of you anger, just as you are'.

A **Analysing**: 'I see that things are not as I would wish them to be' or 'What is the real problem?', 'I notice also: vulnerability, helplessness, confusion, fear … '.

L **Letting go**: 'This too will pass' or 'Just one breath' or 'Letting go'. Offer yourself a gesture of care (see Part 4 if you need some ideas).

Step 2: To someone else try

Firstly acknowledge to yourself if you still feel angry with them. If this is so, then be aware that your speech may well become harsh, exaggerated, loud, malicious, untrue or unkind. It may be useful to let the other person know that you have no wish to act this way and cause further distress to them or to you and that your anger is too strong for a helpful interaction. Perhaps suggest a later meeting or conversation. Take time away and keep practising Step 1.

If your anger has passed, still be mindful for it, and cease the interaction with as much awareness of this as you can if you notice yourself becoming angry again.

R **Recognising**: 'I see that you are angry', 'I recognise that this situation is difficult', 'I see things are not as you would wish them to be', or just stay in the room looking at them – seeing them, breathing alongside them.

E **Experiencing**: 'You are suffering', 'I can see that this is hard for you', 'I am here with you', 'What can I do to help?'

A **Analysing**: 'What else is going on for you?', 'What is the real problem?', 'If I have misunderstood then please correct me', 'And how are things right *now in this moment?*'

L **Letting go**: 'Thank you. Now I understand.' Smile. If you are able, perform an act of kindness (see Part 4).

If an angry situation is simply untenable, seemingly impossible to resolve or just too much to cope with in the moment then the best course of action is often to cease dialogue, if possible to explain your reasons for doing so as non-judgmentally as possible (*I can see we're not getting anywhere right now, this is not helpful, let's take a break for a few minutes/hours/days/years/forever*) and then make sure to give yourself time to reflect upon your emotions, let go of habitual perpetuation of angry dialogue and attend to what may be lying beneath this tough guy.

You may agree with us that it is often more fulfilling and satisfying in the longer term to be kind to yourself (and others) than to always be *right*. Even if you believe that others or the world around you don't deserve your precious forgiveness, remember that you deserve peace. Ask the question: what is hanging onto all this 'finger pointing' in the service of, how is it affecting you, your mood and body right now? How much of your precious time and energy is it consuming? Revisit Exercise 7.1 to help you let go of your anger.

After reading through this chapter and trying some of the exercises, we hope that it is now clear to you that next time anger action rolls into your life you can just let it keep rolling on by without either pretending it isn't there or diving in after it.

Mindfulness top tips to-go

In this chapter you have learned that it is helpful to:

▶ Understand what your anger is up to without getting caught up in it or avoiding it.

▶ Let go of trying to avoid the painful feelings beneath anger as this only serves as a waste of time and adds further stress to your life.

▶ Appreciate that your anger is trying to protect you, which is often perfectly understandable.

▶ Recognise how anger can manifest like a tantruming two-year-old and that it is timely and appropriate to step in as a mindful adult.

▶ Try not to let anger consume you; it makes you inefficient and gets in your way.

▶ Notice your bodily tension and expressions, tone and pace of speech and language when you are angry; is it helping you in that moment?

▶ Notice your vulnerability and need for attention and acknowledgement underneath your anger and aggressive behaviour.

▶ Let go of right versus wrong debates, instead ask yourself how helpful is hanging onto this anger, what is it in the service of?

▶ Forgive others not because you believe they deserve forgiveness but because you deserve peace.

▶ Manage and cope with conflict effectively, carefully and wisely.

CHAPTER

11

Fear and anxiety

Did you ever read the Mr Men books? Well, if so then Mr Jelly is the perfect personification for fear and anxiety – he was nervous about anything and everything. He jumped under the table when his cornflakes crackled, dived beneath the bed to hide from falling leaves and jumped into a tree when a twig snapped – staying there like a great quivering pink wreck shrieking 'calamity!' In fact, he can be very useful to visualise whenever you feel this particular guest knocking desperately at the door for you to let them in before catastrophe strikes.

We are now going to get to know anxiety and fear a little better by:

▶ Helping you to clearly identify them and understand them better.

▶ Noticing how the consequences of acting on them can often be inefficient and unhelpful.

▶ Letting you see that when you are truly present they are not so overwhelming.

▶ Realising that a busy life does not need to be a scary and frantic life.

"Fear leads us to living life in reverse."

Fear leads us to living life in reverse. We plan for what might happen rather than from what is. This is very haphazard and a recipe for disaster really, keeping us hopelessly occupied in seeking every contingency and berating ourselves for our lack of psychic abilities if something unforeseen should upset the apple cart. Also, despite our sense that if we are hyper-vigilant we will protect ourselves from harm, the opposite is often true. Consider this silly, but hopefully illustrative example.

Exercise 11.1: Mindfulness reflection moment

Squashing our world with fear

1 You live on a planet where you can only eat Smarties but ALL the blue ones are poisonous so you take great care NEVER to eat one.

2 Then you hear about blue/green colour blindness, so you stop eating the green ones too.

3 You know that green is made up from mixing yellow with blue, so you stop eating the yellow ones too.

4 Purple and brown might contain blue too, better stop with those as well.

5 You are left with orange, pink and red now.

6 You think you might be allergic to red after a nasty tummy bug, so you best avoid that end of the spectrum too.

7 Now ALL Smarties are dangerous.

8 If you have to survive you need to eat something, but the ability to discriminate has become so diminished you do not know which is really dangerous any more.

9 You either die, or move to planet M&M instead (where you will probably start the whole cycle over again).

The really crazy thing about fear and anxiety is that they are also intended to *protect* us from danger. But we can become so fixated on anxiety-related concerns, especially in our busy, hectic lives, that not only do we lose our ability to effectively discriminate but we are so pumped full of anxiety that we become fearful of even taking time to reflect on what is going on. Act now, think about it never. What can often happen, as we have seen is that these primitive caveman/cavewoman tendencies trigger a lot of adrenaline, which – especially when over-used – clouds our thinking and leads to unhelpful decision-making, not to mention lots of physical aches and pains, which all impede our progress with what we want to achieve in life. So all this panicking, stressing and trying to sort it all RIGHT NOW is actually quite inefficient and tends to shrink our world. We know that many of us feel like we thrive on a certain level of stress, we feel alive and energised. This is exactly the point of adrenaline – it is stimulating, but actually only for relatively short periods, before we end up like Mr Jelly (a quivering wreck) or burnt out. Many psychological studies have shown that certain levels of anxiety and stress actually impair concentration needed for decision-making and reduce the quality of our performance and work.

Because fear and anxiety are physiologically very similar to excitement, sometimes we find ourselves kind of hooked on the highs, which can quite easily translate into lows. Mindfulness is really helpful here in monitoring this. We can tune in to a sense of when 'whoopee!' and jumping from an aeroplane, becomes 'waaaaaa!' because we've forgotten the parachute. Perhaps if we are sufficiently able to let go of the panic we might even find ourselves enjoying the view on the way down.

One possible answer to all this, according to *The Hitchhiker's Guide to the Galaxy*, is 'DON'T PANIC!', if this fails (which it probably will) then try panicking mindfully.

Exercise 11.2: Mindfulness on-the-go

Rush in awareness

1 As you are rushing down the street, racing in your car, trying to catch the last train home through crowds, getting porridge into the baby/cat/self at top speed because you are late, late, late. Just notice.

2 Become aware of your shoulders up by your ears, the tension running into your legs as you walk or sprint, or the strain in your arms as you grapple with the steering wheel or spoon.

3 Take a second to observe your scrunched-up face, your pounding heart, your rapid breathing and sense of impending doom. Allow your experience to be just as it is.

4 Nothing to fix, nothing to make better, no work to be done. Just now, just this moment. Rushing.

5 As you continue to rush on, feel your awareness rushing in, be aware that you are rushing, that's all, nothing more to do.

We have discussed anxiety and fear, but what about when we feel really afraid and frightened? Let's turn toward this now and consider what fear might mean. When we are afraid there is usually a real or imagined threat to ourselves, our loved ones and our sense of physical or psychological safety. The ante is usually turned up when this involves actual physical harm or a serious threat. Sometimes this is extremely handy and prevents nasty accidents such as collisions with pizza delivery bikes, being mowed down by buses, walking off cliffs and playing with venomous snakes. It also (usually) prevents us from telling the boss to stick it, throwing our computers out of a high building and flattening that really annoying person in the office. This is good. We know how well our sense of self-preservation and intelligent ability to appreciate the laws of actions and consequences are working. However, there are times when the fear is so strong that you can smell it (and it really pongs). At these times try the following exercise.

Exercise 11.3: Mindfulness on-the-go

Feel the fear/panic attack!

1 Is this event real or imagined (tip: it's usually imagined as we tend to worry about what might go horribly wrong in the future)?

2 If the event is imagined: this is an unpleasant fantasy or memory. In the case of a very strong experience use an equally strong experience to help you to come as fully back to this moment as you can (have a cold shower, bite on some lemon or a chilli pepper). Now go to Exercise 9.2 in this book and repeat.

3 If the event is real, is the event occurring right now, this very moment in this very place? If no, follow step 2.

4 If the event is real and is happening right now, this very moment, be really honest about any fantasising, remembering, rehearsing or imagining a future scenario and maybe go back to step 3. Remember all you have to manage is just this one moment, no matter how challenging.

   – Focus on your breathing to help you (use the breathing practice in Chapter 3). Ragged, short, fast, shallow, painful, whatever it is, just as it is.

   – You do not need to fix your fear, push it away or ignore it and you can choose to do those things too.

   – Whatever happens the fear will not last, nothing does.

   – You have not always felt like this, you will not always feel like this, just this moment is enough.

   – If you are able to practise like this, keep going.

   – Focus on your breath and let go of holding on to the fear.

   – Allow the fearful thoughts to dissolve by leaving them alone or release the fearful images by letting them be.

   – Keep returning to the breath no matter how often or how strongly you are distracted by thoughts or feelings.

   – Watch the fear changing all by itself.

5 When the fear is less overwhelming: decide if you need to support yourself by acting mindfully to ensure your safety, well-being or that of another. You may need to call for help, leave a dangerous situation or take another course of practical action. As you do this, or

chose to do nothing further, recognise that being mindful has enabled you to make the best possible choices you could have under the circumstances. If 'this is it' and there is nothing you can do, know that fear will change nothing so you can let go, there is nothing left to fight or flee from. You are then free to accept this moment in the most radical way possible as 'just as it is'.

Mindfulness top tips to-go

In this chapter you have learned that it is helpful to:

▶ Look at the effects of fear and anxiety on your body and how they affect our thinking.

▶ Understand how fuelling our anxiety and stress actually decreases our productivity, concentration and effectiveness and shrinks our time and our world.

▶ Bring awareness to when you are rushing about and anxious; nothing more and nothing less than that.

▶ Realise that we can still be busy without being overly anxious.

▶ Discover how mindfulness can help us cope with very strong experiences of fear and panic.

CHAPTER

12

Grief, loss and sadness

In this chapter we will take a look at:

▶ The absolute inevitability of encountering difficult emotions such as grief, loss and sadness.

▶ How to use mindfulness to help you with these moments, even in a busy life.

▶ The superb benefits of giving grief, loss and sadness mindful attention.

Sad case

Boys aren't supposed to have this emotion. Girls are, but only if they don't wear mascara. Sadness often gets pretty squashed – *Don't cry! Crybaby! Silly me! Soppy sod!* Anger is a bit more acceptable, especially in public, and it looks cooler, but take a closer look and there is probably sadness too. And so we might see that we have been trying, or are trying to turn our sadness into something else: anger, confusion or helplessness. It is uncomfortable.

Just like anger, this one needs a lot of care, because here is our soft, vulnerable cry baby. So sweet and tender; but we will never access this while we are harsh, critical or blaming to ourselves or others, no – sadness will hide away. *Phew!* you might think, it's best avoided – let's stick with the macho stuff please. But we know your secret (and ours) – this is the soft spot; this sadness is our Achilles' heel, our 'weakness', we have found the Kryptonite! We guess yours is something like *I am not good enough, I can't cope, I am stupid, no one wants me, I am crazy*, which all equals *I am unlovable*. So your secret is that you think no one will/should/could love you.

> ❝Recognise the powerful, habitual responses of our thinking mind when we feel our soft, vulnerability touched. ❞

But before you leap to the therapist's couch to blame mummy, let's just remind you that we are using mindfulness to deal with the present, not the past. So instead, notice when these thoughts, emotions and sensations of sadness arise. Recognise the powerful, habitual responses of our thinking mind when we feel our soft, vulnerability touched. Notice how anger often comes rushing out in defence. Who wants to admit vulnerability especially in the face of a bullying lion like anger? So we bring up more anger to fight off the bullying in ourselves or others or we flee – and so activate once again our caveman/cavewoman tendencies with the flight or fight mechanism and keep up the adrenaline. If we want to evolve beyond the Stone Age we need to try something else. Stop this fighting and running away. Sit in the lion's den with your anger, face the fear, soften into sadness, because all the attention you pour into yourself with this mindfulness is the antidote to your suffering, it is the answer to your biggest misery and suffering. And do you know what the great paradox is? It is your misery, your suffering, sadness and vulnerability; your great fear of being unlovable that *makes* you so adorable.

> **❝**Sit in the lion's den with your anger, face the fear, soften into sadness. **❞**

Exercise 12.1: Mindfulness reflection moment

There's something brewing ...

1 If you're feeling sad, or suspect that sadness is lurking, make yourself a cup of tea.

2 Place a teabag in a cup and add about a tablespoonful of hot water.

3 Allow to cool a bit and take a sip.

4 What is the taste? Bitter, unpleasant, unpalatable?

5 This is the experience of sadness and pain too.

6 Add more hot water.

7 Add the milk, sugar, gin or whatever.

8 What is the taste? Bearable, sweet, soothing?

9 This is the experience of mindful attention and care of your pain.

10 Go ahead and quench your thirst.

By just paying some mindful attention to our pain, to our sense of vulnerability and being unlovable we can find that it is actually quite bearable (and even loveable). Well, that is what Meera discovered as you can see in the case example below.

Meera

Meera: (crying) Who would want me? Look at me. I am so sad and broken.

Psychologist: Have I told you the story of the broken pots?

Meera: What?

Psychologist: OK, so it goes a bit like this: Every day a lady goes to the well to fetch the water, it is a long walk and she carries two pots on a heavy yoke across her shoulders. One pot is whole, the other is cracked. The cracked pot is sad as it notices how hard the lady works and how it is letting her down by not holding the water. It says to her one day, 'Please throw me away, I am no good, I am broken'. The lady says 'But, sweet pot, you bring me such joy, have you not noticed how the flowers bloom along your side of the road?'

Meera: Are you calling me a crack-pot? (laughs)

Psychologist: Yes, and that is so precious. You are human and I recognise that, I know what that means. With your tears I see your vulnerability and it touches me. Look at me now, leaning forward towards you in the chair. I am engaged. I feel connected.

Meera: But that is just you.

Psychologist: OK, so there you go again. It doesn't matter if I love you or not, or if I am connected to you or not, if you can't accept yourself as you are. So no wonder you feel so lonely. Are you rejecting yourself because you don't feel whole? You expect someone else to want you when you don't even want yourself. Even if they did want you, why would you trust that if you don't believe you deserve to be loved? It leaves you feeling so isolated and alone and unloved. Just like now, here ...

Meera: But ... I do want to be loved.

Psychologist: Yes, that is not the problem is it?

Meera: No. I want to be loved for being a whole pot, but I'm not I am broken and I want to be fixed.

Psychologist: And you are not fixed.

Meera: No. I don't want to be sad.

Psychologist: I know, and you are, let's just sit with that for a moment and breathe.

With mindfulness we give the sadness some attention; we name it and notice it, we recognise it. We see the brokenness and vulnerability, which we have spent so long racing away from and busying ourselves along with a 'just get on with it' attitude. We notice the way we have rejected our pain, denied it while we jump into tasks and chores. But now see, that just by giving ourselves some simple attention, a cup of tea (and – go on – a biscuit too), so to speak, we can bear this experience of heartache, longing, loneliness, helplessness and sense of our unlovableness and with this attention we offer love. And then we can let this go, we can allow it to pass as and when it inevitably will.

Grief and loss

Grief is the melancholic of our guests. Sadness cloaks this one. When grief strikes us suddenly and unexpectedly it is a shock, and even when she sneaks up seen in the shadows of long illness or old age we can find her familiar face still catches us unawares. We can also grieve for lost opportunities, lost youth, money or possessions. Every day, in our busy lives we might notice our losses, even in little ways with not enough time for this or that, or some regret; the too tight trousers, the mouldy yoghurt at the back of the fridge, the missed calls, lunch-breaks and rapidly passed weekends. Some everyday losses can feel even greater; the missing out on that bonus and work promotion or even the loss of our jobs that we had poured so much of ourselves into. Then the winter comes, leaves fall from the trees, friends, family, lovers come and go. Sadness can pervade our lives as we see this endless cycle, particularly when we come into contact with a significant loss.

❝When grief strikes us suddenly and unexpectedly it is a shock.❞

This is a piece of a story about someone in a state of shock and grief and their use of mindfulness at that time, this is what she wrote:

> **Lucy's story**
>
> My best friend's boyfriend has just been killed in a sudden and tragic accident. She has just texted me telling me she is on the way to the hospital with his parents to identify the body. She described this as a 'living

hell'. There is nothing to say, nothing to make this one change, to 'make it better' or turn back the clocks with 'if only' or 'why'. When death comes like this there are no more chances to say 'I love you', or to resolve the wounds of our past; a life is simply swept away leaving behind a great gaping hole of grief. As a friend, all I can do is to be there. This too is the role of mindfulness. I hold the aching form of my sorrow with tenderness and let myself crack. There is no correct way to 'behave', I am, numb, angry, disappointed, despairing or quietly sad by turns, sometimes none of these. No choice but to ride this wave.

Try the following practice whenever you like, paying attention and offering acceptance to your loss and grief, no matter how small or large this sadness feels try this exercise to acknowledge and be alongside this sadness. You might like to use the audio guide to assist you in this practice:

Exercise 12.2: I haven't got time for this practice

Reflective mindfulness

▶ Give yourself a quiet space to sit in stillness.

▶ Allow the grief to come, as it may, in waves.

▶ Open up to this washing over you, as you also open your heart to this suffering, that connects all living beings.

▶ Keep returning to your breathing to ground you in the present, in your life, here and now, just as it is.

▶ You may like to mindfully read some poetry to help you deepen this connection, for example:

> Sometimes I sit quietly,
> Listening to the sound of falling leaves.
> Peaceful indeed is the life of a monk,
> Cut off from all worldly matters.

Then why do I shed these tears?

I'm so aware
That it's all unreal:
One by one, the things
Of this world pass on.
But why do I still grieve?

Ryokan, 1758–1831

▶ It may be helpful to remind ourselves 'this too shall pass'. Allowing emotions to come, letting them go as we gently still the mind.

" We can return to our point of contact with the present, our point of engagement with life, over and over again. "

It can be a jarring experience, when we meet with grief, that the world continues on. The Earth continues to turn on its axis, the sun rises, people continue with their activities, there is still washing up to do, etc. However, it is also these activities, this continued rhythm of life that can help to bring us back again. So while we need to take time to accept our grief with tenderness we also need to, eventually, begin to find our contact point for re-entry into life. We need to recall that spring will inevitably follow winter, that we can re-engage and that there is still joy to be found. This can take a lot of time (that is fine) and it can be accompanied by guilt and doubt (see Part 4 for further help with this). Just like other practices in mindfulness, we can return to our point of contact with the present, our point of engagement with life, over and over again.

Below is an extract about a father whose 16-year-old son died suddenly in a tragic gun accident. He describes the place of mindfulness in his grieving.

> During the day I observe a variety of thoughts. 'I can't do this any-more … my life isn't worth living; I failed as a parent'… All the while I attempt patiently to return to my breath. I forget, and return. I go away with my thoughts and return. I notice my impatience, and return. I see now that underneath the thoughts and the emotions, under-neath the sorrow, the emptiness and all my grief there is something else. It is the absolute unconditional love that I have for a beautiful young man whom I simply miss very much.
>
> In Myla and Jon Kabat-Zinn, Everyday Blessings:
The Inner Work of Mindful Parenting, pp347–8

Good grief

When we see below the pain, distress and agony of loss, it may be that we discover something more, something that tells us about our purpose, our deep connection to others, to our planet or to our commitment to ourselves. For example, the ending of a relationship can be very painful, and yet, perhaps if we seek deeply we may also find our fragile and loving desire to care for others and to be cared for too, we may find our deep wish to be well, to be happy and to feel safe. Then, alongside the pain of this loss, we also see what is most important to us, our true heart, one that longs to connect, one that misses or has missed that chance with this person, or that part of our life, and knows the pain of it. This desire is bigger than death or endings, because we continue to mourn the loss of connection in spite of the absolute inevitability of it. In other words, we all seek, desire and need human contact, attention and care and yet all of us will one day die, all the relationships we have will cease or change. Grief is the emotion that reminds us of our connection to others, that reminds us that even with these fragile feet of clay we have an infinite capacity to love (please refer to Part 4 for an expansion of this). To love and to lose are two sides of the same coin; one cannot come to be experienced without the experience of the other.

A word of caution – watch yourself if you find you begin to use mindfulness as a way to avoid life. The notion that mindfulness practice can be a way to be immune, aloof, cut off or removed from grief is misguided. It really is a form of denial, stuckness and arrogance telling us that we are 'above' this need for contact with others, this 'neediness', somehow superior to it. We may tell ourselves that loss is 'the will of God' or that 'life is just a dream', or it was 'meant to be' – such platitudes actually delude us that we can hold such pain at bay. Seen in others they can be, frankly, humourless and beyond the pale. A friend calls this tendency in him his 'inflatable Jesus', he described how another friend, who was getting some patronising and sanctimonious advice from him, in hushed and reverent tones, about his feelings of loss and the great tapestry of life, turned to him and told him to 'f**k off!' then they had a good old laugh, bursting his arrogance in one fell swoop, and bringing him back to humanity with a comical bump.

So remember this guest, the morbid, solemn-faced character with a chill touch and you may find the scent of springtime on her breath or even that, as you go to sit in contemplative mindfulness, she quietly places a whoopie-cushion on your seat.

As we have seen, mundane daily tasks continue even in times of distress and the presence of painful emotions. It is important to try to not become consumed by struggling with these difficult feelings but to find our contact point with reality while we allow this pain to come and go as it naturally will anyway. It is important to remember that we don't use mindfulness practice to distract from any pain, but we can become aware of our experiences as a way to let go of any struggle with that pain.

In the next exercise you are invited to try being mindful of an everyday activity that you would usually continue, despite what pain may be around for you (if you listen to your dentist, at least twice a day). You are going to brush your teeth anyway, so now do it mindfully. You may like to use the audio guide to assist you with this practice.

Exercise 12.3: I haven't got time for this practice

Brushing those pearly whites

1 Stand in your bathroom. Pick up the toothbrush and observe the subtle movements of your hand knowing just what to do in order for this to happen.

2 Put toothpaste on the brush. Notice the shape of it, the colour, the change in weight, the smell.

3 As you put the brush in your mouth, notice how your whole body, especially your mouth responds to the taste.

4 Begin brushing and marvel at the sounds, movement of your tongue around your mouth, sensations of the bristles.

5 Be aware also that whatever difficult emotion is around for you, this moment you are simply brushing your teeth and need pay attention to nothing else.

6 Recognise also that you are engaging as fully as you can with this gesture of self-care, this mindfulness.

Mindfulness top tips to-go

In this chapter you have learned that it is helpful to:

▶ Recognise that grief, loss and sadness are part of our lives in an infinite number of ways and we can and do cope with them – and this is amazing in itself.

▶ Acknowledge these emotions and see them as part of being human and being alive.

▶ Notice that these emotions no matter how painful tell us what is so important to us as human beings.

▶ Realise that you *can* continue to use mindfulness when these, or any other difficult emotions arise.

Part 3 summary

In this third part of the book, we have shown you that:

▶ All things including our emotions will change and go (and come again).

▶ We do not need to be still, quiet, peaceful or happy to practise mindfulness.

▶ No matter how busy you are, you can make a purposeful effort to notice your emotions in any given moment, the 'good' and the 'bad'.

▶ Trying to eradicate difficult emotions just causes you to become busier and more stressed and unhappy.

▶ There are deeper feelings beneath your busyness and stress that we try to escape from – this causes more busyness and unhappiness.

▶ Sometimes our resistance to difficult emotions is actually a major factor in maintaining them and if we just got out of their way then they could leave all by themselves.

▶ This gracious side-stepping allows a kind of ease about life and all the sh*t we find ourselves in from time to time.

▶ Whether we like it or we don't, we are in it anyway.

▶ We can plan endless acts of avoidance, cunning solutions and crafty takeovers – but we will end up back in reality eventually, and perhaps even realise that we never actually left at all.

▶ Many of our least desirable experiences may actually be telling us what we need, what is important to us and what we are trying to avoid.

▶ We need to stop attacking our human experience and if we are willing, try to find a way into our lives and not a way out of it.

Next time one of the party poopers comes trip-trapping over your bridge, why not invite it in for a tea and a chat? Everyone is welcome here!

In the next section of this book, we are going to illustrate to you all the wonders and beauty that will arise for you as a result of all your hard work – here come the really great pay-offs!

Part

4

Mindfulness and appreciating life

How to come up smelling of roses

This part of the book is about:

- Recognising what and where happiness really is in our busy lives.
- Appreciating life and allowing gratitude and thanks.
- Committing random acts of kindness.
- Finding care and compassion for yourself and others.
- Allowing yourself to be joyful even among all your busyness.

Allowing the good times to roll

If only we'd stop trying to be happy we could have a pretty good time.

Edith Wharton

In this chapter we are going to look in more detail at the effects of:

▶ Grasping after what we believe to be things or events that will 'make' us happy.

▶ Being preoccupied with holding on to 'good' moments.

▶ Being preoccupied with avoiding pain and 'difficult' moments.

▶ Using mindfulness to enable us to cease this habitual, inefficient and distressing behaviour and freeing us to discover genuine well-being.

The big-dipper rollercoaster ride

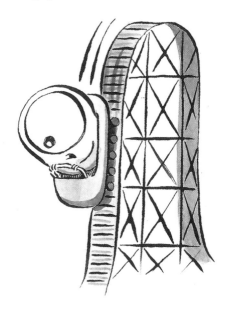

How many times have you longed for your weekend or holiday to begin, only to find that once it's begun you are not enjoying it as much as you'd anticipated, feeling anxious as you count down the days, minutes until its inevitable end and you're right back at work? What about feeling sad and alone being single, anxious that you won't ever meet anyone and longing for a partner to take that pain away, only to find that once a relationship is underway, you are scared and worried that your partner may leave you or that the 'grass may be greener' with someone else? (Argh! Please put the toilet seat up/down – would you!)

Clinging hard to positive emotional states that come from events such as weekends, holidays or being in a relationship while simultaneously remaining fearful and averse to negative feelings such as those associated with going back to work, or being single or 'stuck' with a partner who annoys you, is human and understandable, but often results in an emotional rollercoaster effect in life. The truth is that our emotions change, as do our life circumstances, so having a strong attachment to a situation or event and the inherent positive feeling that comes with it, is going to result in frustration and disappointment every time, leading to soaring highs and plummeting lows in your mood. Take a look at Jackie in the case example below, she clung to positive experiences and struggled with negative ones – ultimately these ways of being caused much upset for her and brought about the exact reality that she feared and wanted to avoid.

Jackie

Jackie felt that if only she had a partner then her life would be 'perfect'. She had a career as a successful litigator in a reputable city law firm; she had friends (who were all in relationships themselves), a home and a close relationship with her parents, but no family of her own. She longed to be in a relationship and felt very sad and low in mood the more she ruminated on the fact that she was 'alone' and single. She became increasingly anxious that she would never meet a partner and instead live a life as a spinster with her cat. When Jackie finally met someone through an internet dating website, her mood rocketed sky high, she was elated and ecstatic and it wasn't long (about one week to be precise) until her thoughts turned to fantasies about the picturesque future of this relationship. She began to imagine and secretly plan her wedding, looking into reception venues and possible honeymoon destinations. She decided at this time that all her problems were over and that she no longer needed to attend any further therapy sessions. It was about four weeks later when Jackie telephoned again to make another appointment. Sure enough, the relationship had not worked out and she explained that her now ex-partner had found her too clingy and preoccupied with worry that the relationship might come to an end. She was beside herself with grief and sadness.

Waking up to and letting go of our natural tendency for attachment to positive feelings as well as our aversion to our negative ones means that we may come to experience more:

- Emotional stability and balance in our busy life.
- More clarity of mind to get ahead and move on the things that are important to us.
- More of the reality we want for ourselves.
- If we are unable to do this, we may find ourselves feeling a bit 'sick of the ride' (pass the bucket please).

Attack of the sleeping zombies!

How truly awake and alive are we really to our lived experience when we are bustling around in fear, clinging and grabbing at positive events and feelings and remaining averse, pushing aside negative events and feelings, as we go? Along with the increasing feelings of low mood and anxiety that arise when we maintain these ways of being, another fact is certain: we seem unaware and almost oblivious to other experiences in our lives. Preoccupations with avoiding feelings of busyness and stress and those lurking below, ones of low self-worth (failure and rejection), mean that we miss out on any meaningful experiences in life that would, no doubt, actually give us satisfaction in abundance. In fearful autopilot mode, we miss opportunities to move on the things that are important to us and that would actually help us to get ahead with living a more productive, rewarding and satisfying life.

So, in allowing our old caveman/cavewomen habits to override our minds, bodies, motives and actions, we run the risk of an unsatisfying existence, to say the least. In this modus operandi it is as if we are blundering through life 'asleep', absent from much that goes on in our lives, absorbed in primitive fear, much akin to a population of zombies! It is important that we wake up and show up to our lives, as they will continue to tick away whether we are present and connected to them or not. We can assure you that with the transformative power of mindfulness you will be showing up to your life more often, reaping and enjoying the varied and numerous rich fruits it has to offer you.

Strangely it can be a real challenge, especially in our Western, busy lives, to actually allow ourselves any genuine pleasure. As we have seen, many of us spend a lot of time uneasy, 'looking over our shoulders' or second-guessing the next dilemma in a defensive position, readying ourselves to deal with and solve the next problem that arises to avoid any further painful feelings. At times this inherent survival mechanism or *problem-solving mode of mind* is consciously apparent to us, say when we notice our attention is caught up in regretting the past and worrying about the future or when others notice and remind us that we are doing the same (all too often). But more likely it is working away in the background of our awareness going unnoticed as it does so.

It might only be a build-up of adrenalin in our bodies, our heart racing, a sudden feeling of anxiety or a deflated low feeling that reminds us of the fact that our protective primeval tendency has been ticking away subtly and quietly in the background of our minds, predicting the next threat coming from either or both our external and internal worlds. This tendency is energy zapping and draining. It can often lead to painful experiences as it fuels depression and anxiety and certainly creates an unfulfilling and an increasingly dampened down experience of life. Our busyness may increase as we distract away from these difficult feelings and we can then find ourselves in a worse place than ever as we struggle to concentrate, to achieve our objectives and manage with any real kind of efficacy. If pleasure can even penetrate this fog of anxiety, often we don't even really know how to savour it, and instead already mourn the time when it will be gone, or worry about grasping it a bit harder and thus end up squeezing all the joy from these beautiful times and ending up in a miserable downward spiral.

Finding ease with life's ups and downs

Grim stuff all this. So here's the good news ... letting go and accepting life in a state of ease and openness is not a very common experience for many of us, and yet it is actually a very natural state for us to be in and we love it. We find that by dropping the judging or evaluating of the worthiness of something (job, relationship, our bodies, ourselves in general, etc.) then our experience of life becomes more and more about just being there in the moment, and that brings a great ease to our lives, whatever else is actually going on. When we recognise painful emotions and see them as a fundamental (and natural) part of life, we see that it is pointless (in fact impossible) and ineffective to fight or flee from them (the truth is that you can't pick and choose which emotions you want – you can try, but our guess is that if you've attempted this, it hasn't actually been that helpful and hasn't made for an easy ride). As a consequence of this realisation we are free to experience a deep kind of relaxation, even alongside our difficulties. This is both mentally and physiologically healthy, as many studies into mindfulness have now shown. There is an increasing body of research (yes, we know we have told you this already, but we're geeks and love this stuff) just highlighting what we are telling you, that mindfulness:

▶ Improves our memory
▶ Helps levels of concentration
▶ Enhances creativity
▶ Increases the speed at which we process information.

But other studies (wait for it, you haven't heard this yet ...) specifically on kindness, gratitude and developing compassion show that enhancing these can also improve our health, well-being and level of functioning. In fact we are going to show you (as if you hadn't cottoned on already) that the qualities of kindness, empathy, self-appreciation, gratitude and compassion *ARE* mindfulness. Also, that these qualities occur *because* we accept our difficult emotions and our vulnerabilities and not in spite of them. It is this very quality of acceptance and, perhaps even more so, willingness to accept life as it is that leads us ultimately to being free from unease and so to being at ease. When we are at ease, we experience a fundamental sense of well-being; we feel joy, contentment and peace in our hearts. This is not a giddy, grasping euphoria where everyday life seems bland and mundane by comparison. This is the realisation that the bland and mundane are nothing of the sort, that what appears ordinary is actually rich, sweet and delicious (it is also part of the deal, it's part of our life). We then know that all that poo that we've been in is actually this fantastic fertiliser for all this great rosy stuff to come springing up out of, and if we didn't have one side of the coin, we couldn't know the other.

> The tiny seed knew that in order to grow, it needed to be dropped in the dirt, covered in darkness, and struggle to reach the light.

> **Sandra Kings**

The crazy paradoxical thing about this is that without pain we wouldn't know pleasure and that it is actually only our own mind discriminating one from the other anyway. Take Marmite, love it, hate it, whatever. Marmite is just extremely salty black stuff (or so our very own extensive scientific investigations have shown), whether you like it and it gives you pleasure or you hate it and it gives you pain is totally subjective. This is the same for anything.

Exercise 13.1: Mindfulness reflection moment

Yin-yang, thank you mam

Have a go at thinking through the answer to the questions below:

▶ Do you say pot-ate-toe or pot-art-toe?
▶ Is the cup half empty or half full?
▶ Is this a picture of an old lady looking down or a young lady looking away?

▶ Are you on the top of the world or on the world's bottom?
▶ What is the sound of one hand clapping?
▶ Was your mother always right?
▶ If so, who was left?
▶ Is the answer to this question yes or no?

We know, stupid quiz you might say, and we'd agree, but add that it does illustrate that all these questions and concerns about good, bad, right, wrong, nice or not nice can bog us down and we can get carried away in trying to figure it all out instead of just rolling about in life with a willingness to savour all it has to offer as each new moment unfolds. This is essentially joyful, like a puppy rolling about in the grass.

To help you along with this we have another handy acronym. This time it is EASE:

E **Embrace**: everything, nothing more, nothing less, all experiences.

A **Accept**: just this moment, this experience as it is.

S **Simplify**: no need to interfere, struggle, work it out or evaluate it, let it be.

E **Exhale**: you can keep breathing (notice how when you are tense, full of anticipation or struggling with effort you often hold your breath and this can increase physical and mental 'up-tightness', when we exhale we naturally relax slightly and let go).

This is about reminding ourselves of how we can live a more fulfilling and effective life. These ways of being remind us that no experiences are outside of our capacity for embracing and living our lives fully. That rushing around or sitting on a mountain-top are all essentially in the same pot of our existence, even if we discriminate and judge and crave or push away, we can't get out of this anyway. We hold lots of beliefs about things, many based on probability – there will probably be weather tomorrow, the world is probably round, Elvis is probably dead, and so on. But really, we don't actually *know* anything. Something will probably happen next, but we don't know it, so why get so fussed and fuddled over it all, trying to figure it all out just so some other smart ar*e can come along and then say 'nice one about the sun revolving around the earth, love the pretty drawings, but – probably not'. So we see how things come into being and go out, this thing is flavour of the month and then it's that one. This just happens whatever we do or don't do, this is just as it is. Simple. And so breathe out …

When we come to appreciate this as reality – that life is 'just this', and only in those moments, do we realise that we can make REAL choices, because we are freed from our habits, caveman/woman tendencies and knee-jerk reactions. As Carl Rogers, a famous psychologist once aptly said: 'The curious paradox is that when I accept myself just as I am, then I can change.'

Love, love, love

If you like the Beatles or Noah and the Whale you can sing along now. This is the moment all you hippies have been waiting for, but before everyone else turns away in embarrassment at those dodgy trousers, wait a minute!

Exercise 13.2: I haven't got time for this practice

Smiley-face face

We have already mentioned the body–emotion feedback loop in the last section of this book (at least twice). But we really think this is amazing stuff, so we're prompting you to try this again now.

1 Whatever you are doing just smile.

2 You can make this easier for yourself by pretending to read something amusing in this book, Kindle, on your phone or computer if you like.

3 Lift the corners of your mouth up gently, allow the forehead to smooth and lift the eyes be soft – go on …

4 See how you feel.

5 Allow yourself to embrace all this experience – nothing more, nothing less. Accepting it just as it is.

6 Simplify the moment by leaving any thoughts, images or memories to themselves.

7 And remember to exhale.

We have a sneaky suspicion that you may have found that OK Because emotions and facial expression are closely linked you may have even enjoyed that exercise. By trying this exercise you have also given yourself a moment of attention, awareness, openness to an experience, willingness to engage, an expression of interest. These are all actions of love (and mindfulness). As we mentioned in Part 3, if you had not been shown these qualities by your parent or caregiver you would possibly not have survived infancy and certainly never have learned well, struggling much of your life with mental, behavioural and emotional difficulties. If you are still having trouble with the link between mindfulness and love, which could be considered interchangeable, then look at this:

> ## Genie
>
> Genie is the pseudonym of a feral child who was the victim of one of the most severe cases of abuse and neglect ever documented. She spent most of her first 13 years of life locked inside a bedroom, strapped to a child's toilet or bound inside a crib with her arms and legs immobilised. Genie's abuse came to the attention of Los Angeles child welfare authorities on 4th November 1970.
>
> In the first several years after Genie's life and circumstances came to light, psychologists, linguists and other scientists focused a great deal of attention on Genie's case, seeing in her near-total social isolation an opportunity to study acquisition of language skills and linguistic development. Scrutiny of their new-found human subject enabled them to publish academic works testing theories and hypotheses identifying critical periods during which humans learn to understand and use language. During the course of their research, Genie gradually started to acquire and develop new language skills. When funding and research interest eventually waned and she was placed in new foster homes, those skills regressed.
>
> Adapted from Wikipedia

As tragic and extreme as the above case is, it serves well to illustrate the immense and essential power of good attention on our basic levels of development. It also highlights that this damage is, potentially, reversible. Since we have not suffered to the extent poor Genie did, we have not been subjected to the degree of damage she was either. Even if our suffering has been, or is currently, very great, we know now that there is also a very good chance that when we give ourselves and others our mindful, loving attention, we can change. We are now going to turn to some very specific ways to enable us to do this and to help us through the good times and the bad.

Mindfulness top tips to-go

In this chapter you have learned that it is helpful to:

▶ Notice that everlasting happiness is an illusion despite what we are told, so stop chasing it.

▶ Understand that you can't eradicate pain from your experience, so best to accept it.

▶ Recognise that grabbing positive and pushing away negative experiences preoccupies our attention and uses up energy and prevents us getting ahead in life; we remain asleep to the beauty of the world around us and the sense of satisfaction within us.

▶ See that mindfulness is the route to genuine well-being in the face of the good and the bad times.

▶ Let go of pain and problem-solving and instead cultivate a sense of ease, that is when you will find well-being.

▶ Be more at EASE.

▶ Give yourself attention and love – it's crucial to your flourishing, progress and well-being.

Rose-tinted roses

The next chapter is focused on seeing life as it is, and this means seeing roses as they are too; allowing yourself to savour the sweetness, offer armfuls to your most beloved and dance in the flower-beds of life (yes, and mind out for the pricks). This little journey will take you on a visit to:

- ▶ Self-appreciation and self-care.
- ▶ Kindness.
- ▶ Gratitude.
- ▶ Compassion.
- ▶ Joy and fun.

You will see that mindfulness brings all of the above and why these are really good for you (and quite nice too).

Self-appreciation and self-care

Chances are that you are reading this wearing something, you may even have washed, eaten, had something to drink, taken any medication you might need, exercised and had some sleep (not necessarily in that order). If you have done any, all or more of these kinds of things you have engaged in acts of self-care. Perhaps you didn't notice this, or are even now dismissing this with a 'Pish! Why of course!' We hope so, because then you are also able to quickly recognise how easily you disregard these everyday activities, how habituated you are to not noticing your frequent gestures of care towards yourself and you know well enough by now that this mindfulness stuff is about noticing all of that and probably more.

It may be that for you, as you fill your life with chores and jobs, possibly often for other people, you sometimes feel underappreciated, disregarded and disrespected. Well, you can't do much about all 'them out there' doing all of that, let them worry about it, because you have quite enough going on. It's time to notice all that *you* are doing, some of it quite miraculously. Anyone with a small baby knows that they and all others like them have achieved *great things* (*especially* if anyone in the household progresses beyond being in their pyjamas all day). If you have worked 4,067 hours in the past week, you recognise the *wonder* that you remembered to eat a piece of toast or brush your hair. But even in lesser circumstances we have done more in a day already than most other species are even capable of and definitely outwit every computer ever invented. Have you ever really thought how fan-bloody-tastic it is that you can even read this?

Exercise 14.1: Mindfulness reflection moment

How amazing?

Perhaps you can spend a moment now, reflecting on anything you can appreciate from:

- the past five years;
- the past year;
- last month;
- yesterday;
- and most importantly – right now.

You might also recognise how you have valued skills such as being able to plan, achieve and succeed. Mindfulness can really help you with these skills as you will improve your mind's ability to focus on one thing at a time with clarity and concentration. It is also totally compatible to the principles of mindfulness to establish or plan for events, activities or ideas that support your intentions in life, just so long as we also recognise that these are very likely to change just as we, and the world around us do too. Kirstin Neff writes:

> Striving to achieve and setting high standards for yourself can be a productive and healthy trait. But when your entire sense of self-worth is based on being productive and successful, when failure is simply not allowed, then striving to achieve becomes tyrannical. And counterproductive. Research indicates that perfectionists are at much greater risk for eating disorders, anxiety, depression, and a whole host of other psychological problems.
>
> *Self-Compassion*, pp70–1

When we adopt an attitude of EASE, perhaps reminding ourselves of this when we find ourselves too caught up in rushing for impossible deadlines, killing ourselves over the latest diet fad or straining to fit in one more rep at the gym, just maybe we can take a step back – seeing everything we're up to as it is, realising it can be quite simple just to let go and exhale into the next moment. We can even appreciate the misguided assumptions of our mind – which are so busy struggling to 'get it right' or 'be better' or 'be perfect' – and remind ourselves that this tactic hasn't been working so well; in fact for all that effort, it is pretty much a dud deal. Why not try congratulating yourself for trying something different, for all the mindfulness practices you have participated in, for all the ways you have already helped create new neural pathways to genuine well-being and success instead?

Self-appreciation can sometimes feel a bit uncomfortable if we have been led to believe that blowing our own trumpet (toot) is somehow vain, embarrassing or conceited. It is helpful to remind yourself that self-appreciation is not about being superior or striving for perfection, it is about noticing and allowing yourself to be free from these things and to fully experience life, and that includes you! Wait a moment, stop and rewind back to the top of this paragraph, here's a louder trumpet sound for you, one for us and one for all of mankind – you know we all deserve it: TOOT, TOOT, TOOOOT! To hell with it, let's get the whole brass band out!

To add to this, do you realise that according to physicists we are made of the same basic atomic components as the stars? American astrologer, Carl Sagan wrote:

> The nitrogen in our DNA, the calcium in our teeth, the iron in our blood, the carbon in our apple pies were made in the interiors of collapsing stars. We are made of starstuff.

We think that that is definitely something to appreciate about ourselves, and also to recognise that without the particles that made us, the apple pie or the universe and all of its infinite mysteries would not be complete. Not only are you matter, you REALLY MATTER

Have a go at the following mindfulness practice, it will only take a few moments and you can do it while you are in the bathroom as part of your morning routine. It may feel a bit odd and uncomfortable at first – but if you're willing to try it, it really is worthwhile. You may like to use the audio recording to assist you with this.

Exercise 14.2: I haven't got time for this practice

Mirror, mirror on the wall ...

1 Whenever you next find yourself near a mirror, preferably in private, stop and take a good look at yourself.
2 Look deep into your own eyes and notice how they shine like the stars (because they really do).
3 Remember to breathe.
4 Notice what thoughts may arise, perhaps judgement, criticisms or appraisals.
5 See if you can let go of the content of these thoughts and, gazing deeply at yourself, marvel at your amazing capacity to have thoughts and intelligence.
6 Looking into your eyes, breathing, take a moment to wonder at your body's wisdom in allowing you to see, to breathe and to be as well as you are (however well that may be), sustaining your life.
7 Take this moment to appreciate yourself in whatever ways you wish. You might even like to try a sneaky smile and see that miraculous person just in front of you smiling right back at you.

Gratitude

> I feel a very unusual sensation – if it is not indigestion, I think it must be gratitude.

Benjamin Disraeli

When we're so busy bustling along in our lives or flying high with our superhero cape flapping merrily behind us (check out Chapter 2 to remind yourself which Busy Superhero you have been trying to be), we can forget gratitude really easily. We often overlook all those chances to be pleased with our lot. This is especially true if it's 'one of *those* days'. The dog ate our breakfast, we missed the bus, the boss is in a bad mood and no matter how much we think of stardust it's just not cutting it. What is there to be thankful for in this? And that's not the half of it, what about being met with a hot, steaming helping of illness, bereavement, redundancy, assault, eviction, bankruptcy, or other threats to our safety or well-being? Then there's some little twit in the way, walking too slow, breathing too loud, playing loud head-banging music and just existing in the wrong way. No one gets how bad it is, no one sees how much you are suffering, no one can help anyway and life is just one big fat disappointment after another. Yeah. Thanks a bunch.

This would be a good moment to reach habitually for the cigarettes, bottle of gin, spliff or choccy biccies. Give the below exercise a go to enhance your awareness of gratitude. You may like to use the audio guide to assist you in this practice.

Exercise 14.3: I haven't got time for this practice

Biscuit bountiful

1 Hold the biscuit in your hand and see it, just this moment.
2 You have this very biscuit to chomp (or crisp, or whatever morsel usually takes your fancy) just as it is.
3 Notice your anticipation of eating.

4 Take a bite.

5 Just let it sit in your mouth for a moment before scoffing it.

6 Feel the taste seeping into your mouth; allow it to permeate your senses.

7 Savour the changes in taste and texture as you chew.

8 Feel the sensations as you swallow.

9 What are you eating, disappointment? A sense of lack? Pleasure? Or something else.

If you want to take this a bit further you might like to consider the following next time you chow down your lunchtime sandwich:

> The silver rain, the shining sun
> in fields where scarlet poppies run
> and all the rippling of the wheat
> are in the bread that we do eat.
> So when I sit at every meal
> with grateful heart I always feel
> that I am eating rain and sun
> in fields where scarlet poppies run.

Alice C. Henderson, The Harvest

Research suggests that practising gratitude is one of the most reliable ways of increasing happiness. This can be enhanced by making a daily record, perhaps in a diary or on your phone or tablet, of things which you feel grateful for. This really helps to develop the 'attitude of gratitude' (that rhymes!). This can include absolutely anything you like – from being thankful for having clean water to drink to recalling the kindness of the person making your coffee (that might be yourself). If you are having a grumpy moment, it might be handy to look at a previous list to inspire you, and then you can add your gratitude now for having done this task (and maybe for even waking up to your grumpiness).

> **❝Research suggests that practising gratitude is one of the most reliable ways of increasing happiness.❞**

As we develop awareness of our gratitude we also see, as a natural consequence, all the very many ways that we become interconnected with our world and other people through it. Just like the poem above, we begin to see the myriad ways in which even a piece of bread is connected to the sunshine, fields, rain and air that contributed to the wheat growing, then we can see that this wheat was collected by a farmer, produced by people in a factory or kitchen, collected by someone, made into a sandwich and then possibly wolfed down in a few mindless seconds by you – unless you catch the chance to be at EASE, to open up to everything, to all this experience has to offer you, right now, just as it is. It is that simple and you can exhale, perhaps some of the very same air that will now travel its way towards some wheat in a field of poppies.

Kindness and generosity

It pretty much follows that when you start to appreciate and be grateful for your life you will find it so much easier to be kind to yourself and others. We know how nice it feels when others are kind and generous towards us, but what is *really* in it for us if we are kind and generous too, apart from looking like a do-gooder, suck-up, teacher's pet? Well, firstly 'suck-up stuff' needs a bit of mindful attention regarding our own sense of self-worth, value and confidence and is not usually a generous act at all – if you think that this is like you go back a bit to the section on self-appreciation above and/or take a look also at Part 3, especially the section regarding 'anxiety and fear'. It's important to notice how not one behaviour is intrinsically helpful or unhelpful to your well-being, it's all about the motivation behind that behaviour, you need to become aware of what that is.

"True generosity takes quite a lot of skill."

True generosity takes quite a lot of skill. If we give too much then we actually deny ourselves, and are dismissing our own needs. A client, Sandra, relayed a scenario, which was a common occurrence, where her mother always served everyone else first and gave herself the smallest, most meagre portion 'one potato for me is fine' she would state loudly and slightly self-righteously – this really got up Sandra's nose (her mother's tone that is, not the potato). These kinds of acts of 'generosity' are nothing of the sort, and we all know that really. They are passive ways of saying 'look at me, I'm so good', although they actually seem to have the opposite effect as we think 'annoying do-gooder' or 'just have another sodding spud would you?' Acts of pretentious martyrdom tend to infer somewhat self-absorbed assumptions about those around us, perhaps that we would think them greedy, selfish or indulgent if they took too much (or even enough), and this can feel quite an insult if we genuinely wish them care.

It is painful to see others not taking care of themselves, and if we know this, we also know that when we don't care for ourselves we hurt others too. When we're too busy to notice this (and we really mean mentally busy), we are often blind to the carelessness with which we treat others. We can get caught in a 'who's had the hardest day' competition with our partners, or bury our head in a book pretending not to see the pregnant lady hanging-on bravely to the rail in the bus, we walk hurriedly past the collection tins, *Big Issue* seller and lost tourists. But do you remember a time when someone showed you a random act of kindness? Maybe they gave up their seat for you, offered you a helping hand, gave you a spare ticket to something, a thoughtful gift or made a friendly comment? Many of these gestures cost us very little in terms of time or money and yet they can make such a significant impact on our day, or even our whole life. As psychologists, we know the precious value that even the simple act of listening to someone can have, even in the direst of circumstances. Many successful retail and service industries make use of this too, recognising that clients and customers like to be treated well, to feel valued and that they are much more likely to return or make recommendations if they do.

If you think you don't have time for expressing gratitude, kindness and appreciation try this following exercise as you go about your days and see how it goes.

Exercise 14.4: Mindfulness on-the-go

Cheers, nice one

1 Make a commitment to say 'thank you' at every opportunity.

2 Try to drop sarcasm and any insincerity, recognise this instead as aspects of possible anger that needs some acceptance and attention all of its own (return to Chapter 10 to refresh on how to manage your answer mindfully).

3 See if you can say 'thank you' with more than just the obligatory passing phrase, can you really feel thankful, if so, you will sound different – go ahead and try it.

4 You can enhance this practice by really looking at someone (their face, not their shoes/boobs/lovely bum) and saying 'thank you, I really appreciate what you have done', 'thank you, I'm very grateful for this/that' or 'thank you, doing/saying x was very kind of you'.

In the times in which we live, simple actions such as a smile or a 'thank you' go a long way. They are usually manageable even when we feel tired, rushed off our feet and/or downright miserable. If you want to crack the icy layer of frost lying over your frozen sense of joy, verve and interest in life, then this exercise can be a really good and easy place to start.

As we worry about the bills, striding past people under cardboard boxes, avoiding the crying children (perhaps even a tantruming two-year-old), with the adverts demanding that we be stronger, faster, richer and more popular (all for a price, of course), then the tension can be seen all over our face and the faces of others. But try a smile, a 'thank you' or some other acknowledgement of another person and witness, at least nine times out of ten, that the frost magically melts. If you are warming to this melting idea (ha ha) then you might like to try some counterterrorism. Really. The ideology of terrorism is one of extremism, it involves intimidation and advocates aggressive acts to achieve its goals. Is this any different, at a grassroots level, to belligerently bullying yourself to 'pull your socks up', 'take it on the chin' or 'man up'? Continuing to push yourself well beyond your physical, emotional and mental limits – to extremes – is not really (ideologically) any different from extremism.

Exercise 14.5: Mindfulness reflection moment

How do you terrorise yourself?

Perhaps you can identify the ways in which you terrorise yourself. These may involve:

- ▶ Criticising and berating yourself regularly.
- ▶ Ignoring your physical and health-related needs (such as sleep, illness or even going to the loo when you need to).
- ▶ Denying yourself pleasurable experiences (such as socialising, preparing yourself your favourite food or having a long bath) because you have something 'important' to do instead.
- ▶ Engaging in unhelpful behaviours such as excessive drinking, dieting, gambling or dangerous driving.
- ▶ Kidding yourself that you are 'dealing' with difficult emotions by pushing them away.

So the idea of counteracting these activities can be considered counterterrorism. This is *not* akin to fighting terrorism, which is, anyway an oxymoron. Leave oxymorons for the morons who like to 'fight for peace'. Instead try being really radical. Arm yourself with your marshmallows, lollipops and jelly-beans and try the following exercise.

Exercise 14.6: Mindfulness on-the-go

Commit random acts of kindness

These can be grand gestures, or small ones, it doesn't matter. There is no need to necessarily save that baby from the jaws of a tiger (you might have to wait a while at the zoo for this) or stop the run-away train that has somehow become a burning missile heading for some very important American building (as this requires lots of make-up and a Hollywood set) – just something teeny-tiny will suffice. You can do these feeling like a total wally or like a saint, they will still work. Here are some ideas, use these, or your own. Start by picking three, do them today or as soon as you can and when you are willing:

▶ Water the plants, feed the cat, play with the kids, phone great-auntie Hilda, have a bath, go to the gym, look out the window for a moment and enjoy the view, listen to some music, complete an unfinished task, leave a task unfinished, give to charity, send someone a cheery text message, buy a gift for yourself or for someone else, clear away the clutter in your home, tidy up, leave a mess, put on some fancy clothes, take them off (woo-hoo!), make love, make tea, take a break, let someone else take a break, etc.

▶ You may also like to crack a smile or make friendly (not flirty) eye contact with a passerby on the street, maybe saying 'good morning' or the like, simply acknowledging their existence.

In these busy times, simple actions such as a nod or smile can have a profound impact on how we and others feel (in a good way). We can do these things even when we feel our most stressed and busy (no excuses). It is actually quite amazing to notice how many of us are looking down, avoiding eye contact as we rush around. No wonder we feel so isolated and alone a lot of the time. Are we scared to let others in, to leave ourselves exposed? What are we hiding? (Part 3 of this book can help to understand.)

If you want to feel more alive, connected and joyful in life, these random acts of kindness can work a treat (we highly recommend them).

> **"** *Happiness and meaning is already inside us all, it's down to our own way of being.* **"**

Take a look at the case example below, to see how such simple acts of kindness can really be quite life-changing and also help us to realise what is really important to us in life.

Alf

Alf was a very successful broker who had been through two difficult divorces. He found that he was at a juncture in life where he had suddenly lost all his confidence, was unsure of his current relationship and his work and questioned what the point of it all was. Despite his wealth and success he felt something was 'missing'. Every day he passed a tramp (we'll call him Ed) on his way to the office. Come rain or come shine, there Ed was, wrapped in a tatty old blanket, with his dog on a string. Alf started to nod to Ed and sometimes say 'hello'. Occasionally he chucked over a bit of spare change. Then one day, after considering the wisdom of giving money to someone who might use it to buy drugs, and not wanting to be party to this, he bought Ed a cup of coffee. From then on Alf started to say 'Hi, how are you doing?' and have a brief chat. One day the tramp replied 'Oh I'm OK, it's my birthday today'. On a whim Alf decided to get him a card. He gave it to Ed, and Ed's eyes filled with tears; he told Alf that this was the first card he had had in 13 years.

Alf was profoundly affected by this interaction. He began to recognise these very such small acts of kindness occurring in abundance all around him. He realised he rarely smiled, said 'thank you' or appreciated even the small things in life. He began to understand what had been missing.

Most of us assume that happiness comes to us from the world around us (that's what we have been led to believe) but stop searching and striving for this to magically appear and come your way, happiness and meaning is already inside us all, it's down to our own way of being – it's up to us to create the reality we want for ourselves. Have a read of this great quote:

When people come to the end of their life and look back, the questions that they most often ask are not usually: 'How much is in my bank account?' or 'How many books did I write?' or 'What did I build?' or the like ... You find the questions such a person asks are very simple: 'Did I love well?', 'Did I live fully?', 'Did I learn to let go?'

Jack Kornfield

Have a go at the following mindfulness exercise, it's a great one to practise being present, enhance awareness and act in the spirit of kindness.

Exercise 14.7: I haven't got time for this practice

Mindful washing-up (also known as 'how to do housework graciously and become adored by all')

This is a practice that can be done with any household task. You can transform your home and yourself with mindfulness! You may like to undertake this practice in the spirit of kindness, allowing yourself to take time to notice each movement as you dedicate it to your housemates, kids, partner or any other being (such as yourself). This way you now have a good few minutes transformed from mumbling under your breath about the inequalities of menial domestic chore distribution, into a tranquil oasis of benevolence. You might like to use the audio guide to assist you in this practice.

1 Undertake this task in silence (the audio guide doesn't count here). If you can, allow yourself some time to do this task.

2 Take a moment to enjoy the bubbles sitting in the warm water, or watch the tap like a waterfall cascading into the sink. Notice the sensations around you of colours, sounds and smells.

3 Treat each dish as precious; as an opportunity to delight in this moment. Just washing each dish slowly, with care and attention.

4 Use the breath to bring you back to the moment if your mind wanders. Allow yourself to pause with the cleaning of the dishes and just breathe once in, once out. Now return gently to the task.

5 Allow yourself to become alive to the moment through your senses.

6 As you wash-up, cleaning each item with care, let your thoughts (like it's not fair, I do everything around here', or the like or whatever else they may be) dissolve in the washing-up water along with the dirt from the plates, cups and cutlery.

7 Be fully present in this act of kindness.

Compassion: brave new world

As we have seen, at the heart of all mindfulness is awareness, nothing more, nothing less. Inherent in this is the acceptance. As we embrace and accept the nature of both our own private experience (thoughts, feelings, behaviour and sensations) and the busy world around us, we begin also to allow life to simply unfold. As we relinquish our delusions of control over life and cease grasping at how things 'should be' to seeing them as they truly are, a kind of veil is lifted and from this we enliven a new sense of interest and curiosity in even the most ordinary events, objects or experiences. Much like a curious archaeologist who may uncover an ancient find for the very first time, with mindfulness we bring our attention to explore our experience, just how it is, letting go of preconceptions, judgements, preference or opinion. We have seen, and you have now experienced, how beneficial this can be as a means of shedding light on our habitual ways of thinking and in learning to understand and accept our difficult emotions in a totally new way. We uncover the treasures hidden beneath the surface of our 'taken-for-granted' life, looking more deeply we are then free to receive the insights and wonders they offer. We see life clearly at last.

"We uncover the treasures hidden beneath the surface of our 'taken-for-granted' life."

Compassion is a particular quality that arises naturally from our clarity and acceptance – often like a rose from the sh*t of our difficult emotions. When we observe how we and those we love (as well as those we don't, or those we feel quite neutral about), suffer from being caught in their struggle to accept reality, then we can look into the very heart of suffering with a kind of fearlessness. When we understand pain and suffering without grasping for something different, nicer or 'better', then we see the very truth and reality of life. We see that we all suffer – from the smallest beetle to a great blue whale, the wealthiest rock star to the poorest street urchin. Without exception, each creature is subject to ageing, illness and death – at the very least. This realisation, while it can be in itself quite painful, also liberates compassion. And now instead of avoiding pain, using mindfulness, we accept the reality of it and alongside this are then able to offer genuine, authentic care to ourselves and others.

This can sound simplistic, or even a bit soft. However to do it you need to be smart and fearless.

Sometimes your only available transportation is a leap of faith.

Margaret Shephard

Compassion requires seeing a situation clearly, directly and thoroughly. A swift and precise cut with crystal clear awareness through our delusions and defences needs to be pretty bold. Let go of your story-telling about busyness, anger, fear, sadness, let go of your craving for something else and you will find that there is compassion.

Try the following exercise, which is about noticing others around you (in a particular way) with compassion. You can do this while:

▶ on the train or bus;

▶ in a café;

▶ walking down the street;

▶ looking out of the window;

▶ looking around the office;

▶ anywhere really where there's people;

▶ or you could even imagine and picture your unforgiving boss, your very worst enemy or the lady in HR that keeps calling you to discuss your return to work (and you're just not ready to yet).

Exercise 14.8: Mindfulness on the go

People-watching

1 Spend a few moments watching the people coming and going.

2 Allow you attention to focus on one person – a man, woman or child.

3 S/he suffers too.

4 S/he struggles with the same types of thoughts and feelings; s/he is human too.

5 S/he gets ill, ages and will die.

6 All of those s/he loves will get ill, age and die.

7 S/he is like you.

8 Say to yourself: 'May we both be treated with compassion.'

(You can replace the last line with something else if you prefer, like 'may you feel joy', 'may we find kindness', 'wishing you well'.)

Our typically busy lives are full of 'urgent demands' and relentless requests for our help, and 'this won't take long, but …' or 'only another few minutes of your time'. It is, seemingly, easy to rush guiltily on by – in fact it often feels necessary, in order to stand even a remote chance of keeping up with everything else. Each apparently innocent request from a charity hawker with a bucket or sorry spiel from a telesales call room is another pull on our already overstretched lives threatening to tip us over the edge.

There is much research to indicate that when we feel under threat we develop defensive ways of coping, which reduce our abilities to care for ourselves or others with compassion – we develop a kind of 'compassion fatigue'. As we have discussed in earlier parts of this book, mental stress and strain puts us in a state of 'high alert' and we respond to this *as if* we are under threat. It is no wonder then that anxiety and depression can be accompanied by a lack of self-care and compassion.

Other people or circumstances can appear to be the very cause of our problems so we can be inclined to keep away or emotionally cut ourselves off. We elbow the charity hawker out of the way or scream cathartically at the telesales person or ignore phone calls and withdraw from loved ones, as we are desperately attempting to defend and preserve our tiny patch of space to breathe. This route can become one of intense isolation, loneliness and despair. We hope you have seen that there is a way back. In fact, the way back is here, now and in this very moment. The second you wake up to this you open to compassion and there you have the antidote. Quite simply, forget about the other people who need your help, want your money, time or that very breath. It might *look* nice and sweet to give them your time, money or breath as you are screaming on the inside, but our guess is that someone else might be needing some good attention right now. If you haven't twigged who that might be yet, try the next exercise to find out.

Exercise 14.9: Mindfulness reflection moment

Give me five

You have five minutes to change the world. These are magical minutes that happen sometime between now and midnight tonight (and if there are four or less minutes to midnight now as you read this – just let that go!). Who are you going to give these five minutes to? These are the scenarios:

1 Just as you struggle in at 7pm with the groceries the phone rings. It is a call from India Rashid is offering you a chance to switch your energy supplier and save you squillions of pounds if you please bear with them for another half an hour of uninterrupted, unintelligible monologue.

2 You have an email from a mysterious and grammatically challenged, but respectable, gentleman in Nigeria offering you part of his winnings in a lottery if you would only forward all your bank details and PIN number right now, as a matter of urgency.

3 An over-friendly student with a clipboard from a charity representing the most pitiful people, abused animals and impending environmental disaster EVER corners you on your 15-minute work break saying 'think of the people/animals/planets you could save with just a bit more of your time/money/breath'.

4 The homeless guy asks for your change to get somewhere to sleep and pleads to give him any spare food, in the same speech he gave you every other time you saw him. He is looking right at you, twitching slightly from alcohol withdrawal.

5 Chatty Kate from the laundrette sees you in the street. She has been having a horrid time with her boyfriend Nasty Neville, oh and has she told you about her neighbour's brother's auntie's cat who was nearly run over by that famous person from the telly whose name you surely must know? And, I know you've got to get on but …

6 Late on in the evening, it's dark outside. There is a careworn person reflected in the glass of the window, just finishing off the last chores, while worrying about how to pay next month's rent and struggling to breathe. Is that you?

So, we think you get the point … We all need care and attention. But we only increase the universal suffering quota if we don't start by giving some care and acceptance to ourselves first. It is simply unhelpful to give any of our time, money, breath, kindness, or anything, to anything or anyone else if we haven't even got enough ourselves. We can also rec-ognise the way that others might play on this by taking advantage of our busyness, gullibility, guilt and actually our desire to make the world better, when we respect our sense of self-compassion and care. Others taking time, money, energy, etc., that we don't have is simply unkind to us, but equally by giving that which we don't have, we can be unkind to ourselves too. Genuine acts of compassion and care are heartfelt – not derived from our autopilot reactions, aversion to difficult emotions or grasping at the 'feel-good factor'. Self-compassion recharges our 'compas-sion fatigue', so we can then become re-energised and re-engaged with the suffering of those around us in an authentic way. In other words; we need to put our oxygen masks on first and breathe deeply before we can help those around us.

A further aspect of compassion, therefore, is how it serves to increase our sense of connection to others. We are all aware of the irony that in our modern-day lives, with the amount of social media that we have at our fingertips and our ability to travel to the corners of the globe, the rates of relationship breakdowns and sense of isolation and loneliness are higher than ever.

❝The more we disappear into our proverbial navel, the more we forget the world around us, and the more alone we can then feel. ❞

Without mindful awareness and the compassion for our suffering that arises from this, we can lose perspective. Our suffering, and consumma-tion with obsessing over trying to 'fix' it, can become very inflated. It is true navel-gazing. The more we disappear into our proverbial navel, the more we forget the world around us, and the more alone we can then feel. Bigger brains than us have figured this out too:

> A human being is a part of a whole, called by us 'universe', a part limited in time and space. He experiences himself, his thoughts and feelings as something separated from the rest ... a kind of optical delusion of his consciousness. This delusion is a kind of prison for us, restricting us to our personal desires and to affection for a few persons nearest to us. Our task must be to free ourselves from this prison by widening our circle of compassion to embrace all living creatures and the whole of nature in its beauty.
>
> **Albert Einstein**

Again, the great news is that we have a LOT of universe around us. Your particular patch may be very full of life indeed. This little microcosm you call 'work', 'home', 'park' or 'planet Earth' is probably teeming with it. All this life busy bustling along on your keyboard, phone, street or in the skies. Every weeny bacteria or bull elephant bumbling about somewhere upon this floating ball in space, probably getting lost in their own navels too (do bacteria have navels?). We are surrounded. Life is right here in our faces and making a right old racket about it. Consider this, when do you ever truly experience silence? Probably the answer is rarely, if ever. Therefore we have another mindfulness practice available in abundance and requiring no special set-up, even in 'silence' we have an experience of the absence of sound. Cars, aeroplanes, trains, the sound of walking feet, phones, babies crying, the old busker trying to sing in tune, the computer humming, a clock ticking, people yakking, birds tweeting, the mystery noise in the night that might be an old pipe, but ... ?

Try this next mindfulness practice of sound now, to enhance you awareness further. You might like to use the audio guide to assist you with it.

Exercise 14.10: I haven't got time for this practice

Stop, children, what's that sound?

1 Just take a moment and listen to all the different sorts of noises you can hear, including the sound of silence between the other noises.

2 Now see if you have a favourite noise. This time listen to this sound.

3 Notice the variations in intensity, volume, frequency, rhythm, tone or absence and presence. Just notice. If your attention is distracted elsewhere, that's OK, just bring it back to your specific sound when you realise.

4 Next take a moment to reflect on any emotions that may be present from listening to this particular sound. There may be no particular emotion, several, or nothing strong – that's fine too.

5 Notice your thoughts also occurring about the sounds.

6 Recognise that *you* are making the emotions or thoughts, not that sound. Simply recognise this relationship between a sound and an emotion and/or thought, be aware that the associated feelings and thoughts are actually not random, they have arisen through your own creation in *relationship* to this sound. Also, just like the sound, the thoughts and feelings may also arise and fall, or increase in tone, intensity or duration.

7 Now it is time to let go of the sound, of the emotion, of the thought. Allow your attention to expand back to include all or any sounds that come into your awareness, see them as freely flowing events arising and falling.

8 Feel your connection to the world through your sense of hearing; know that this may be stretching several miles around you from right inside your inner ear. You are part of this. Reach out and embrace this moment.

Joy and fun

Generosity, kindness, compassion, yeah, now we have it. Fun! School's out kids – time to re-enact that scene from *Grease*. Come on, we wouldn't really expect you to practise wrapping your arms around your inner child and hugging people in telesales if it wasn't going to be fun would we? At least *sometimes*. No we wouldn't!

Speeding through life like a hamster on amphetamines gets really exhausting. There is just no energy left after a while, no matter how many push-ups you do, how much coffee you down or the number of times you beat yourself with a stick. Eventually you will drop. We have looked (in Part 3) at how to do this with a little grace, and we've told you a bit about coming up smelling of roses and now we're going to see how you can get up, put those roses between your teeth and shake your booty.

As Westerners we don't have a bunch of funky monks throwing us one-liners about the meaning of Zen just around the corner when we are having a bad day. We are not often in the vicinity of a free mountain-top or ashram in which to 'find ourselves' before we dash back to work. But, we think you probably realise by now, that for the sake of waking up to life, that doesn't matter. If you are waiting for the next bus to Buddha-ville, then take a seat on your here and now and do some mindfulness, because that bus will only lead you back to this spot anyway.

You're not going to figure it out. There isn't anything to work out at all. And that is the great cosmic joke! The punchline to this life, that we look so very serious about working out, is probably something like an approximation of the probability of calculating the statistical likeli-hood minus the square root of quantum theory. Huh? Exactly. There is no punchline. So now we are free of that great load of hooey, now what? Well, how about taking a good look around this great bowl of life-stew you are sitting in? Time to wake up and become aware of your world.

> **"You're not going to figure it out. There isn't anything to work out at all."**

Being aware, with this new energy and concentration uninterrupted by meaningless, painful craving and grasping, can become quite power-ful. You can be free from all that cluttered, unproductive, busy thinking and focus fully on simple moments. Not only can you be more efficient, focused and less stressed, you are now free to *really* enjoy a cup of tea or coffee, the sound of a car rumbling past, the face of a stranger or a con-versation with a loved one.

> The most precious gift we can offer anyone is our attention. When mindfulness embraces those we love, they will bloom like flowers.
>
> **Thich Nhat Hanh**

In our busy lives many of us have been primed from an early age to pick flaws, criticise and problem-solve, so we need extra practice at enjoy-ment. We then really come to appreciate all the gestures we make to ourselves and others on a daily basis; our acts of generosity and kindness are *noticed*. The world takes on a different hue and it is rose-coloured a lot more of the time than perhaps we ever knew – no need for spectacles. The colour of our life now is one in which we are no longer 'taking-for-granted' what and who we have around us – including ourselves. We can be free to fall back in love with our world, our partner, our work, our bodies and/or our innate love of adventure. All the distress trapped by our unmet needs in the past becomes liberated and transformed by our awareness and with it come other qualities such as joy, carefreeness and playfulness.

As children, most of us loved simple pleasures. You may recall lying in the grass and watching the clouds, building dams in streams, playing football with your friends, collecting stones or stickers, skipping and running – just for fun. You might even remember times when you saw or did things for the first time, your first look under a rock, the first time you learned to ride a bike or your first kiss. Life can be like this now, when we open those innocent big eyes of ours (no matter what you've seen before) and look at the playground we have in front of us. As adults, most of us even get the big toys and games to play with – like cars, real money and sex. We can make decisions and choices about where and when we go and with whom. And sometimes, especially when we are having a tough day, we might like to remind ourselves how to play by going to a comedy show, watching a kid's film, eating chocolate by torchlight under the duvet, buying sweeties or blowing bubbles in the park.

So come on, let's start the party, right now! Have a go at this next mindfulness practice, this is where the fun really starts.

Exercise 14.11: I haven't got time for this practice

There may be bubbles ahead ...

… but whilst there's moonlight and love and romance, just blow the bubbles and dance.

1 Get hold of a bottle of bubbles.
2 Hold the bottle in your hand. Notice any emotions, memories or thoughts.
3 Open the bottle and mindfully grapple the little wand out of the inside.
4 See if you have a film of coloured mixture in the loop ... or you may need to get one.

5 Hold the wand up to your mouth and notice any anticipation to blow, see if you can let it go and be fully here, just as it is.

6 Breathe in and out, blowing gently into the loop. Be aware of how you may be gunning for a big bubble, or a stream of lots of little ones. Watch what comes, or doesn't.

7 You may like to watch the bubbles drifting and popping as you release them into the world. Just like your thoughts.

8 See how, as you give yourself up to each moment, you can open up to the simple pleasure of now.

Mindfulness top tips to-go

In this chapter you have learned that it is helpful to:

▶ Wake up and notice your habits of self-care.

▶ Notice your achievements and amazing abilities as a human being – appreciate yourself not because you are better than the rest but just because you *are.*

▶ Express more gratitude, it is proven to increase happiness and will make you feel connected to others.

▶ Be kinder to yourself and others, you will find true meaning and satisfaction in these acts of kindness.

▶ Notice what motivates your acts of 'generosity' – is it self-worth and fear or genuine kindness?

▶ Be less self-critical and harsh with yourself.

▶ Commit random acts of kindness; they really help to enhance our sense of well-being and connectedness.

▶ Notice others with compassion – we are all in this together and suffering in the same way; compassion leads to a greater sense of connectedness and well-being.

▶ Care for yourself before others, otherwise you'll have little left to give.

▶ Practise having fun, being carefree – space for this will arise when you let go of problem-solving and trying to work it all out all the time.

Part 4 summary

In this part of the book we have explored ideas about what the 'good life' actually means and come to understand more fully that happiness arrives in a more genuine way, a more profound and centred way, when we use mindfulness. We can now understand that:

▶ Our struggle with pain is a fundamental part of being able to appreciate ourselves, and to develop kindness, gratitude, compassion and a sense of community, as well as joy.

▶ Far from being soppy, these qualities are essential for our physical and mental health.

▶ It is possible to foster kindness, self-appreciation, joy and compassion through very simple exercises, many of which you may do already, requiring no additional time demands. Others are simply quite fun and may have a great additional pay-off worthy of investment.

We have also highlighted that there is plenty of research supporting our suggestions, and more coming to the fore even as we speak, let alone a tradition of several thousand years behind the concepts we have outlined (more of this to come in Part 5). We also now have shown you several suggested ways in which you can continue to enhance your mindfulness skills in your busy, modern-day life and allow the roses of your mindfulness success to fully blossom.

But we're not finished yet, we have a quite few more helpful tips, insights and exercises to share with you in Part 5.

Part

5

Mindfulness and moving forward

Parting shots

In this last part of the book we are going to:

▶ Remind you how your awareness is infinite and abundant, with you always in every moment.

▶ Show you how you'll know that mindfulness is working for you.

▶ Tell you what you can do when it feels like mindfulness isn't working or is too difficult to practise.

▶ Help you to see why mindfulness is so popular and why it is very important to us all now in this modern world.

▶ Give you some suggestions for further reading and useful contact pointers.

But before we do all that, we would like to remind you of the journey you have embarked so far upon. This has taken us through:

▶ Understanding what mindfulness is about.

▶ Seeing how mindfulness can free us from the seemingly impossible dilemmas of a busy life.

▶ Understanding and developing a different relationship to our difficult emotions.

▶ Allowing fun, kindness, compassion, gratitude and self-appreciation to flow back into our busy and stressful lives.

As we have seen, these monumental shifts occur, not from continuing to rush, physically or mentally from one place or idea to another, but rather from a quality of inner stillness and a state of being present with life, just as it is. Instead of feeling buffeted from one experience to another, we discover the constant, and that is the boundless expanse of our very own *awareness*.

CHAPTER

15

No full stop

In this chapter we are going to:

▶ Again notice how our awareness is with us always.

▶ Show you what you can do when you feel mindfulness isn't working for you.

▶ Illustrate what you can do to ensure that it does work for you.

▶ Remind you how to notice when it is working for you.

So here we are, this is the final part to this book but no need to fret, why so sad? Or are you relieved? Perhaps you are wondering if this mindfulness is actually working or not? Can you master it? Is it clicking into place? Any feeling is fine really (just acknowledge it, there it is). Know that you can go right back to the start whenever you want or any other chapter that you desire (we hope that you will continue to revisit parts of this book) over and over again. Be aware that, just like this book, your awareness isn't going anywhere either; you can be aware whenever you want. Mindfulness is always with you, beauty is everywhere and we hope that by now you are starting to see that.

> "Be aware that, just like this book, your awareness isn't going anywhere either."

Awareness is abundant

Let us remind ourselves of this abundant awareness. The Western, or Westernised, modern world in which most of us live today is hectic, demanding and relentless. With endless advancements in technology, unsteady economies and terrorism to contend with, we also attempt to balance time for work, friendships, relationships, children and 'leisure' time, to take care of money, families, housing, health and mental well-being, and somehow to remain relatively sane most of the time. This is combined with living alongside the realities faced by any living being, the fundamental suffering that we all experience, of ageing, illness and death. Even in the absence of anything exceptionally difficult in our lives, and especially when things are tough, it is an absolute miracle that there are still smiling faces, birthday celebrations, loving embraces and many random acts of kindness and generosity occurring every minute of every day.

> "We have an absolute abundance of these opportunities to become more aware."

As Westerners in a hectic world, we have an absolute abundance of these opportunities to become more aware and it seems vital that we create more of this kind of space for ourselves (especially when we are ducking, diving and side-stepping so much coming at us from every direction all the time). Compared to our yogic friends in their mountain-top retreats, we may consider that we have ten times the opportunity to bring attention to this very moment, to be awake. To be alive to this moment, to give it our attention, is to make it grow, and life can begin to transform from one of lack (where we may not be noticing much, we are half asleep or consumed with unhelpful narratives about the past or future) to one of blessings, rich and fertile, our life becomes *alive*.

> There are only two days in the year that nothing can be done. One is called yesterday and the other is called tomorrow, so today is the right day to love, believe, do and mostly live.
>
> **Dalai Lama**

The great thing is, that if we miss this moment (with the rare exception that our lack of awareness leads us to be run over by a bus), we have another opportunity, the next moment, and then again and again and again.

Awareness is the part of your mind that does not change for the entirety of your lifespan; it is always there often in the background as you rush around contending with your busy life. It holds the ability to simply *notice* and acknowledge (but not think about) your experience, thoughts, feelings, behaviours and sensations. Awareness is the 'missing link' (or the one we forgot about), it is the very thing that can help us cope, it creates the necessary space for us that we long for, that we need, in this fast-paced, information overloaded existence that we have created for ourselves (more of this to come a bit later).

> ❝*Your busy existence and the world around you changes but your awareness that notices these changes never changes.*❞

Your busy existence and the world around you changes but your awareness that notices these changes never changes – it remains constant and the same. Your awareness has been with you since the day you were born and will be with you until the end of your time, it is always with you in every moment, it's with you right here and right now as you read the final pages of this book (as it was when you started to read this book and it will be again when you come to revisit it at a later time). Let's not lose touch with it anymore.

Exercise 15.1: Mindfulness on the go

Awareness is now

Take just a moment again now to tune into that experience of awareness:

▶ The sensations of holding this book (or Kindle, or whatever device you may be reading this on).

▶ The weight, textures.

▶ The sense of space around you.

▶ Perhaps also notice any particular thoughts arising, or any emotions or urges to move or other sensations.

▶ There! You just dropped in (we told you that your awareness is always there – watching your back).

Awareness is much like the sky, which is always there. Whatever occurs in the sky, whatever weather, or storms pass through, the sky remains undisturbed and unchanged. Your awareness is just the same, whatever thoughts, feelings or sensations you experience, they come and go, they pass through your awareness, which is left intact thereafter as solid, firm, stable and secure as it ever was.

It's pretty likely that as you read this now you no longer are aware of the sensations of holding the book (Kindle or whatever) that we asked you to focus on just a moment ago – this is because you are now paying attention to what you are reading. This awareness also reminds us that all the experiences that you have whether in the form of a thought in your thinking mind, a physical sensation in your body, a feeling in your emotions or a way of behaving or performing will always come and go again, as if they were clouds passing by in the sky of your 'awareness'. We can now appreciate the futility of grasping at these experiences and how impossible it is to get anywhere from doing so, except possibly more stressed and exhausted.

> If you realise that all things change, there is nothing you will try to hold on to. If you are not afraid of dying, there is nothing you cannot achieve ...
>
> Lao Tzu

Nevertheless, we do need to engage some degree of effort to focus our attention on the present, particularly in very challenging circumstances or when these ideas are quite new. This effort is not about attaining the prize for the biggest mindfulness powers ever, it is actually more about the effort of letting go and reminding ourselves that even if we had such a prize, it wouldn't make us happy, better or safer anyway. You already hold the answer to all your problems, keep observing, dropping into awareness and this will become clearer to you.

> You, the richest person in the world, have been working and struggling endlessly, not understanding that you already possess what you seek.
>
> **The Lotus Sutra**

So, are you now ready to let everything and everyone else know that they are off the hook? Are you really ready to open to the truth and embrace being fully responsible for your own happiness?

> I think it's very healthy to spend time alone. You need to know how to spend time alone and not be defined by another person.
>
> **Oscar Wilde**

If not, then why not? Well maybe you are struggling with all this a bit too much.

It's not working

So how do we actually know that mindfulness is working and what do we do when it isn't? Well, our answer is, just breathe, try it, see for yourself, how is this very moment? Now, this one? Can you let the future unfold like this? Can you let go of having to control the outcome, can you trust yourself this much?

> **"Worrying whether mindfulness is or isn't working is only going to stress you out right here and right now."**

When we focus too much on the outcome (*when will this mindfulness thing work, already?*) we are not here in the present but rather there (or then!) – worrying whether mindfulness is or isn't working is only going to stress you out right here and right now. (Is that you trying to work it all out again, desperately trying to get it right, using mindfulness as a 'control' strategy to ensure you get to that perfect place of bliss? See we told you this wasn't easy.)

> A mind that is always comparing, always measuring, will always engender illusion …
>
> **Jiddu Krishnamurti**

As we outlined at the start of this book, if we develop an attitude of openness (acceptance) as to whether we do or do not reap the benefits of mindfulness, we are in a much better place to notice the fortunate by-products of regular practice arising. Flowers open without us forcing the buds and we can also trust that things will happen at the right time naturally. This is about coming to appreciate and live with the 'what is' rather than the 'what if?' The truth is that all the benefits of mindfulness that you want are already within you – you are already relaxed, efficient, creative, an excellent decision-maker, productive and at peace – it's all there and working just fine, but fretting that this stuff will never come, that's what gets in the way of this and actually clouds your vision to this reality. You got it now?

You get there by realising that you are already there.

Eckhart Tolle

So here are some tips for when you find that you are trying just that bit too hard and expecting this all to work faster, better – now already!

Exercise 15.2: Mindfulness on-the-go

The Goldilocks principle

Try the following when difficulties arise with being mindful as you go about your busy days. So if you're finding that …

▶ It's too hard – *yes, and this is a moment that is hard, be mindful, breathe, this too shall pass.*

▶ I don't understand – *yes, and this is a moment that is confusing, nothing to work out, nothing to fix.*

▶ I can't do it – *yes, and this is a moment of struggling, nothing to get 'right', just as it is.*

▶ I am so happy, I just couldn't practise – *yes, and this is a moment of happiness, breathe, this too shall pass.*

▶ I'm so miserable, I just couldn't practise – *yes, a moment of unhappiness, breathe and let go.*

▶ I'm really good at this, I've got it! I don't need to practise anymore – *a moment of clarity, this too shall pass.*

▶ This mindfulness porridge is too hot, too cold or (shock, horror) all gone! – *this moment, whatever it is, is as it is, nothing more, nothing less.*

Honest, this is not a cop out – you manage the above and you will find relaxation, calm, spaciousness, contentment, ease and peace. Let go already! Mindfulness is a solution that you can bring to any of life's problems and it will bring you positive results. Just let go and see for yourself.

By golly this is great!

When you abide in the moment, in your awareness, life's richness is revealed. At times mindfulness can give us clarity, awareness and insight with the speed and precision of a lightning bolt and it can knock us off our feet.

> **When you abide in the moment, in your awareness, life's richness is revealed.**

Often mindfulness is a clumsy affair, we notice something and then drift back to our habits, then we realise this, go 'oh, duh!' and promptly do it again. As you know by now though, this does get more instinctive, and the quality of experience can become a little more subtle. With practice we recognise the nuances of our own mind's little habits, its particular hamster qualities and foibles.

The more real you get the more unreal the mind gets.

John Lennon

Periods of ease can become gradually prolonged as we are now attentive to life's usual pitfalls, and when we fall off the wagon, we realise that there wasn't really a wagon to fall from anyway and sitting on our posterior in the dirt is just where we happen to be right now.

Therefore there is no full stop. We said no full stop. No. Stop … (grammar, eh?). We don't attain a 'level' of human superiority and then get to rest there feeling smug. You might feel filled with the bliss of the holiest of holies doing mindfulness, but you still have to fill out that tax return later. You may be bowled over with grief, and you still need to feed the goldfish. Life just goes on unfolding.

Life just offers what it offers, and our task is to bow to it, to meet it with understanding and compassion. There are no laurels to acquire.

Jack Kornfield

Yes, you guessed it; this is an ongoing journey for us all. Mindfulness is not to be attained and completed, no certificates will be awarded here. It's a practice for life, in and out of awareness we go, cultivating and reinforcing the same. And by golly it is all so very worth it.

"Mindfulness is not just for the stressful times."

Some of the most common utterances that we hear from our busy clients are: *I don't need to practise right now, I feel great!* Or *why is this not working, I'm so stressed and it's just not helping?* We understand why we might not feel the urge to practise when all is rosy in the garden, why fix something if it ain't broke, hey? We get this, we're the same. But, what's your purpose in taking your car to the garage for a MOT we'd ask? Mindfulness is not just for the stressful times, it's a way of being that if you practise (when you are feeling fine and dandy too) will help you out when you need it the most. So don't expect it to magically appear or work a treat when you feel like the world is crashing down around you and you can't see a way out. It's a discipline – practise, practise, practise is the key. But know that it does get easier and before you know it awareness will arise more naturally and with more clarity and frequency.

Try not to see mindfulness as yet another set of garden shears that is annually pulled out from the cobwebs of the garden shed to extract those pesky weeds, you may find that they're a bit rusty and too blunt. Nurture your awareness every day, as much as you can and that way you'll find that it is more naturally to hand when your garden is overgrown and those bothersome nettles need attending to. Likewise, when the sun is out and the flowers are in full bloom, you will find that you actually notice this, and may even take time to sit back with a beer in the deckchair and soak it all up.

It may feel strange, frustrating, and the rest, at first (and then again) when practising this new way of being – but remember that this is absolutely normal and these experiences are a gateway to mindfulness too. Peace, relaxation and well-being are products of the mindfulness work that you do, try to focus on them less and they will arise more naturally.

Exercise 15.3: Mindfulness reflection moment

What's showing up?

Over time, as you have continued to practise regularly, have you noticed:

▶ Clarity of mind, improved concentration and focus?

▶ A greater sense of ease, peace, relaxation, stability (despite how busy you are)?

▶ A greater sense of productivity, efficiency with your daily tasks?

▶ Improved communication in your relationships?

▶ You are more free to make the choices that are helpful to you to get ahead in life?

And if you haven't, then let it go, don't worry about it – be mindful … and then as soon as you do this, as sure as night follows day – there you have it – clarity, freedom, peace and tranquillity (and then they too pass again, and return, and pass …).

Mindfulness top tips to-go

In this chapter you have learned that it is helpful to:

▶ Remember that awareness is a constant source of stability, expansive and always there.

▶ Know it is the key to finding some space and tranquillity in these increasingly hectic modern times.

▶ Recognise that we have an abundance of opportunities to become more aware in this Westernised world.

▶ Acknowledge that awareness is the space within which we can stand still, at peace in this stressful world.

▶ Make an effort to focus your attention when times are tough and mindfulness is new to you.

▶ Try not to worry whether mindfulness is working or when it will work, this only takes you away from now and will only stress you out.

➤

▶ Notice that you are already at peace, efficient, productive, relaxed and creative, fretting that you may never experience more of this just gets in the way of you seeing all this existing in you already.

▶ Know that practising mindfulness can feel clumsy, you will move in and out of awareness – and that's fine.

▶ Remember mindfulness is not just for the stressful times, it's best practised when you are feeling fine, that way it will be to hand when you need it the most.

▶ Bring awareness to your struggles with practising mindfulness.

Mindfulness in the real world

In this chapter we are going to:

▶ Remind you how you can best fit mindfulness into your busy life.

▶ Show you how you can continue to be mindful alongside your busyness and stress going forward.

▶ Recognise why and how mindfulness is so very popular, relevant and important to us now in these busy modern times.

Although mindfulness may conjure up images of beautiful yogis sitting in the lotus posture, smiling benevolently in the sunset on picturesque mountain-tops, we hope by now that we have shown you how it's not all about this at all.

Sure mindfulness began in the ancient East and is a specific practice of Zen Buddhism (from Japan) but the word 'Buddha' actually is an ancient Pali (from the Indian subcontinent) word, which literally translated means 'awakened one'. It is traditionally used to refer to a specific man, but it could as easily be anyone who is 'awakened'. 'Awake-ism' (or Buddhism) is therefore totally interchangeable with any other religion, ethic, doctrine or system that leads to an experience of 'awakeness'. Religious beliefs, a belief in God, goddesses or gods and/or an afterlife are neither incompatible, nor necessary. Zen as a strand of Buddhism is itself very down to earth and pragmatic – it *is* essentially a practice of mindfulness, present-focused, realising the here and now, just as it is. Mindfulness goes back further (no doubt) thousands and thousands of years, and we also know that other cultures and traditions have been waving its flag for centuries too. Take Ancient Greece for instance, doesn't this all sound a bit mindful to you?

It is the mark of an educated mind to be able to entertain a thought without accepting it.

Aristotle

We have learned from ancient history how to bring this all into our modern world, no ancient text or practice originating from these historic times indicates that we need to be in another time or place to practise or benefit from mindfulness – we have been handed down very simple instructions, all the tools we need are right here with us right now. All we have to do is recreate this ancient tradition and practise it in our modern Western world, we don't need to change our world to fit this practice and that is what this book has been all about. Mindfulness is as relevant today as it has always been – and maybe even more so, especially when we think about how *busy, buys, busy* and stressed most of us are. Maybe this is exactly what we have all been missing, ignoring and longing for (for far too long).

> *Mindfulness is as relevant today as it has always been – and maybe even more so.*

Busy mindfulness

We have illustrated to you how being busy without reflection, awareness and mindful attention is the cause of more busyness and stress in our lives. Busyness on its own is not the problem here, it's our relationship to it. When we carry on with our busyness, 'blissfully' unaware, ignorant to our ability to be aware, we miss out on so much of our life, causing ourselves more stress, busyness and taking less satisfaction from it all; we lose sight of our true purpose. With awareness maybe we can just allow ourselves to simply be BUSY (nothing more and nothing less than that):

- B Being awake and aware to our busy experience and unhelpful busy habits.
- U Unhooking ourselves from struggle with stressful thoughts, feelings and sensations.
- S Stabilising ourselves, by making contact to this present moment with acceptance.
- Y Yielding to the needs and ways of being that bring more meaning and satisfaction to our lives, ourselves.

Our busy world in all its glory

We live in a world that is stressful and painful; you will be busy, you will experience heartache, loss, fear and stress if you're choosing to take part in this thing we call life. The choice is yours. Know that if you are not willing to accept this suffering (and we do mean truly accept) then you won't really be taking part at all and all your efforts to escape what you don't want will lead to more suffering.

> *Working towards not feeling bad just really equates to not feeling at all!*

For too long we have assumed that the answer to our pain is to work it out, to problem-solve and push pain away – hit the 'feel good' button and keep it firmly held down in place. But we're only kidding ourselves with this and we continue to buy into this farce via the media, Hollywood and new technology. We work on this premise; that we must feel good and not feel bad, but working towards not feeling bad just really equates to not feeling at all! You know this by now and that this doesn't work – there is no way out of your pain, only a way into it to truly gain some genuine freedom and relief.

Exercise 16.1: Mindfulness reflection moment

Hey, I feel good, I knew that I would(n't)!

So what is your purpose with all this feel good stuff, is it really working for you? Ask yourself these questions:

- What is the cost of expecting and wanting to feel good (and not bad) all the time?
- How does this affect your mood in general?
- Your progress to get ahead in life?
- Your relationships?
- Health?
- Finances?

No doubt all your attempts to feel good and not feel bad ever, are not working for you very well when you consider the above.

The truth (as you also know all too well by now) is that we can't change the way the modern world is and the experiences we will have as we bustle through it, so stop expecting and trying to. When you reject your experiences, your feelings, your suffering, you are truly rejecting yourself – your feelings and experiences become disowned and lost. Are you really prepared to turn away from yourself, no matter how hard it might be to face this suffering, in your hour of need? We cannot guarantee anyone else will be there for us, even with their best intentions. But you are right there and have been all along, you are still with yourself now. If not you, then who? If not now, then when? It is important to offer yourself this kindness and compassion (mindfulness) if you want some warmth, care and stability (even if it is just for one moment) amidst this often cold, judgemental and hostile world. That is how you might make this stressful experience that much more bearable, more satisfying and manageable and come to experience all of it in all its glory.

So, are you willing, are you now ready to let all your experience in, knowing that your struggle to push parts of it away is just making you busier and that it ultimately will burn you out (if it hasn't already that is)? Remember that if you are not willing to have these painful experiences then you've probably got them anyway (amplified)! So, don't just say you will accept all this pain, can you really, truly accept it, know that you suffer too, just like us and just like the next man and woman, and that is OK? It is life – you are really no weaker for it – you are HERE AND ALIVE after all. The greatest challenge in our life may be to discover exactly who we are and then our second is to be happy with what we find. Mindfulness is a wonderful tool to do just that.

> To measure you by the smallest deed is to reckon the power of the ocean by the frailty of its foam. To judge you by your failures is to cast blame upon the seasons for their inconstancy.
>
> **Khalil Gibran**

So if you are not ready to leave this place and time just yet (yippee, its great to have you aboard to share the ride), why not try to reflect on the following questions daily, they will help you to see the wood through the trees and keep you on track as you go.

Exercise 16.2: Mindfulness on-the-go

Willing and able

The questions to ask yourself are:

- ▶ Am I willing to step into my life experience and fully engage with it all?
- ▶ Am I willing to take all this busy world has to offer along with me for the ride?
- ▶ Can I let go of the 'what if?' and see the 'what is'?

▶ Am I willing to hold my pain and suffering with dignity?

▶ Am I willing to invite my pain in, take care of it and pay it kind attention?

▶ Am I willing to act boldly, make a difference even when it feels so difficult to do so?

▶ What do I offer myself, this world, if I run away from my experiences right now?

▶ What is my purpose here, right now?

Think of yourself as dead. You have lived your life. Now, take what's left, and live it properly.

Marcus Aurelius

Now is the time to wake up and wise up

As we have seen, mindfulness is growing in popularity in so many contexts of our lives. The evidence base for its effectiveness in helping us to manage this stressful world and all our aches and pains in it is substantial and growing at a very fast rate indeed. We know that mindfulness has been around for centuries so this begs the question: why is it becoming so popular right now, in these modern times?

Well, we just have to look around us to find the answer to this. It is probably the exact same reason that led you to pick up this book in the first place. We find ourselves yearning, hankering after an antidote to all the stress and busyness we experience in these modern times. Mindfulness is indeed very timely.

❝Mindfulness is indeed very timely. Our human mind did not evolve for this modern world.❞

Our human mind did not evolve for this modern world. It was designed to protect us, to take in as much information as we could, to second guess our downfall, to see the worst around us, to problem-solve – yes, we will survive! Yet, in these modern times we have information flying at us from every direction all the time at an alarming rate. We like to multitask. Most of us are plugged into one or more devices at the same time, checking emails while surfing the web, following the Jones' on Twitter,

TV on in the background, music playing on our iPod, answering texts on our phone – oh and yes dear, how was your day?

We have so much to process and a lot of this information is scary stuff too. You only have to turn on the TV, log into the news, open a newspaper for a few minutes to hear, read all about the cataclysmic disasters and global infections that are out to get us. The collapse of our economy, the mass hysteria – my goodness, will we survive? I don't know, will we? But what if … ? Our minds are programmed to work all this out, to fret to protect us in the face of such hazards and catastrophe. Like a computer, our minds are ready for the next upload of data, all too happy to fill up any empty space with the next constant barrage of pain and suffering to work out. We then lose ourselves; we lose contact with who we are, with others, sucking in all this information overload, in our attempts to keep safe and sound. Oh the irony – we then become psychologically exhausted, burnt out and distressed. It is not surprising that an escape to another peaceful place and time begins to sound very attractive indeed.

But where can we really run to? Where can we take ourselves to avoid all this pain and suffering? A large glass of whiskey, maybe? Yes, that will do the trick! No, then how about another sleeping pill or to hell with it, let's just spend our savings and book that trip to that faraway land – I need to get out of here, like now already! But no, we cannot turn on ourselves in this way; we can't escape and turn off our very own minds and run away to an imaginary Shangri-la. Is the answer to turn this all off, to live a 'perfect' life, returning to the land of milk and honey and dance in circles of joy? It may be. However, this 'utopia' will be unsustainable if what we actually are *really* doing is running away from reality. We know by now that we create our own reality from how we *think* about and *relate* to the world around us. If our mind's habitual way of working is struggle, denial of reality, grasping and pushing at life, we will find stress and distress whether we're up to our eyeballs in modern gadgetry or attempting to 'live the simple life'. Turning off, tuning out or dropping out work equally as well as turning up, tuning in and dropping in to – if we use mindfulness. When we are mindful our reality is revealed. We can then make mindful choices (join the Amish, carry on as we are, buy a new TV) and these will naturally support our deepest intentions for ourselves – whatever those may individually be. And as our awareness unfolds, with mindful attention, so these choices may change, just as we continue to, just as our world does.

"When we are mindful our reality is revealed."

There is no full stop, the world is developing, growing, changing and we need to develop and allow our minds to evolve too to keep up, to prosper and flourish and enjoy this wonderful creation of ours – the modern world, and ourselves as part of it, just as it is, just as we are, moment to moment.

Bringing mindfulness practice along with us, into our busy, modern-day lives, in any form that works for us, enhances our awareness of the reality of the world we are creating for ourselves. We gain insight into this, we find clarity, effectiveness, creativity, kindness, joy and wise up to it all with awareness.

We then cultivate minds that are ready and allow us to cope with this world; our very own splendid creation. We need to offer ourselves back this gift, create a place in this world, a place to stand within it, to feel firm and strong amidst the crazy busyness and stress that we continue to bombard ourselves with. Let's wake up and be kind to ourselves – allow ourselves to truly enjoy this new wonderful creation of ours – mindfulness is this space from which we can. The awareness gained through mindfulness is the space within which we can then create more space. This space is large enough to hold it all; the crazy busyness, the peaceful stillness, the grief, the joy, the hamster mind, the tantruming child, the man made of stardust, the iPhone, the whole universe and the kitchen sink – all of it.

Exercise: 16.3: I haven't got time for this practice

Mind the gap

1 Spend a moment noticing thoughts arising.
2 Let go of the content and attend to the space between thoughts.
3 Become aware of this gap, even if fleeting.
4 Notice that in this gap is spaciousness.
5 Allow yourself to experience inner space.

> Every time you create a gap in the stream of mind, the light of your consciousness grows stronger. One day you may catch yourself smiling at the voice in your head, as you would smile at the antics of a child. This means that you no longer take the content of your mind all that seriously, as your sense of self does not depend on it.
>
> **Eckhart Tolle**

The mindful warrior (NOT worrier!)

So, can you continue to take what you have learned from this book into your real world with you? Can you find your inner strength, lean into your wise and abundantly spacious mind and let it help you find the way? Can you live boldly and continue to do what you care about, what is important to you with courage alongside the pain that you might feel when doing it? You mindful warrior you!

The choice is yours. We hope that we have helped you to see, to experience how strong and powerful you really are, how you have all the answers to a less busy and more peaceful life inside of you already. Look inwards – there you are.

> The search for truth and understanding is a journey that ultimately leads one to the true source of oneself.
>
> **Benjamin Greene**

> Your vision will become clear when you look into your heart. Who looks outside, dreams. Who looks inside, awakens.
>
> **Carl Jung**

Using mindfulness enables us to create space from our busyness and stress, meeting them also with understanding and compassion and bowing with awareness. Practising mindfulness, with intention, is a way in which we can train our minds to return to awareness, which is our natural and authentic state of being.

" In order to transform yourself, you need do nothing other than be where you are right now. "

Using the insights and exercises we have shown you within this book as often as you can will help you to reinforce the fundamental principles of mindfulness as a way of being. You have seen how this can happen in any and all situations, busy or otherwise. In order to transform yourself, you need do nothing other than be where you are right now.

> In the end, these things matter most: How well did you love? How fully did you live? How deeply did you let go?
>
> **Gautama Buddha**

Mindfulness top tips to-go

In this chapter you have learned that it is helpful to:

▶ Know that mindfulness is not new to us, we have always known it and how helpful it can be.

▶ Recognise that we have all the tools to practise mindfulness already, with us right here and right now.

▶ Understand that mindfulness is as relevant today as it has always been and maybe even more so when we consider all the stress and busyness we contend with.

▶ Simply be BUSY without adding more busyness and stress on top of that.

▶ Try not to feel good all the time, as this just equates to feeling nothing at all.

▶ Notice if there are any costs of trying to feel good all the time, in terms of your mood, well-being, productivity, relationships, finances and health.

▶ Be willing to accept all your experience, pain and suffering too, hold it with dignity, care and attention.

▶ Recognise that mindfulness is now very timely and crucial to cope with these modern times.

▶ Understand that mindfulness is the space in which we can stand to allow ourselves to enjoy our very own creation – this modern world.

▶ Be mindful as you move ahead in your real world – act boldly and wisely.

Part 5 summary

In this section we have:

- Revisited our awareness and learned how it is central to mindfulness.
- Looked at the pitfalls of practising mindfulness and how you can overcome them with mindfulness.
- Illustrated how you can continue to take mindfulness with you into your busy life.
- Highlighted why and how mindfulness is so crucial to us in these modern times.

You may wish to now (if you haven't already) look up our audio files at www.pearson-books.com/mindfulness. We would also like to point you towards some additional reading and some ways of further enhancing your practice, which you can find listed at the very end of the book.

We do hope that you have enjoyed reading this book as much as we have enjoyed writing it. We have discovered and learned so much. We wish you well on your journey ahead, may you experience joy, may you experience peace and may you experience a rich and meaningful life.

> By sharing something, I realized that I'm not alone, that there are a lot of people that share with me the same preoccupations, the same ideas, the same ideals, and the same quest for a meaning for this life.
>
> Paulo Coelho

Thus shall we think of this fleeting world;
A star at dawn, a bubble in a stream;
A flash of lightning in a summer cloud,
A flickering lamp, a phantom, and a dream.

from 'The Diamond Sutra', an ancient Buddhist text,
the earliest written copy of which dates back to 868 BCE,
translation found in *Teachings of the Buddha*, p141

Recommended reading

▶ Alidin, S. (2010). *Mindfulness For Dummies*. John Willey and Sons: West Sussex

▶ Bond, F. W., Flaxman, P. E., Livheim, F. & Hayes, S. C. (2013). *The Mindful and Effective Employee: An Acceptance and Commitment Therapy Training Manual for Improving Well-Being and Performance*. New Harbinger: California

▶ Brach, T. (2003). *Radical Acceptance: Embracing your Life with the Heart of a Buddha*. Bantam: New York

▶ Dali Lama (1999). *Ancient Wisdom, Modern World: Ethics for A New Millennium*. Little, Brown and Company: London

▶ Gerhardt, S. (2004). *Why Love Matters: How Affection Shapes a Baby's Brain*. Routledge: London

▶ Gilbert, P. (2013). *Mindful Compassion*. Robinson: London

▶ Harris, R. (2008). *The Happiness Trap: Based on ACT: A Revolutionary Mindfulness-based Programme for Overcoming Stress, Anxiety and Depression*. Robinson: London

▶ Hayes, S. C. & Smith, S. (2005). *Get Out of Your Mind and into Your Life: The New Acceptance and Commitment Therapy*. New Harbinger: California

▶ Kabat-Zinn, J. (2004). *Wherever You Go, There You Are: Mindfulness Meditation for Everyday Life*. Piatkus: London

▶ Kornfield, J. (2000). *After the Ecstasy, the Laundry: How the Heart Grows Wise on the Spiritual Path*. Bantam Books: New York

▶ Rezek, C. (2012). *Brilliant Mindfulness: How the Mindful Approach Can Help You Towards a Better Life*. Pearson: Harlow

▶ Salzberg, S. (2004). *Loving Kindness: The Revolutionary Art of Happiness*. Shambhala Publications: Boston, MA

▶ Suzuki, S. (1973). *Zen Mind, Beginners Mind*. Weatherhill: New York

▶ Tich Nhat Hanh (1991). *The Miracle of Mindfulness*. Rider Books: London

▶ Tolle, E. (2004). *The Power of Now: A Guide To Spiritual Enlightenment*. New World Library: San Francisco

▶ Williams, M. & Penman, D. (2011). *Mindfulness: A Practical Guide to Finding Peace in a Frantic World*. Piatkus: London

▶ Wilson, K. G. and DuFrence, T. (2010). *Things Might go Terribly, Horribly Wrong: A guide to life liberated from anxiety*. New Harbinger: California.

Further useful contacts and support

▶ City Psychology Group, mind-blowingly fantastic mindfulness workshops, therapy and lots of other goodies from your delightful authors and their colleagues: **www.citypsychology.com**

▶ Independent mindfulness information website: **www.mindfulnet.org**

▶ Free, downloadable podcasts on mindfulness and more: **www.zencast.org/**

▶ More downloadable talks and information about retreats: **www.dharmaseed.org/**

▶ Free, downloadable mindfulness bell for your PC or laptop: **www.mindfulnessdc.org/mindfulclock.html**

▶ Great information on mindfulness, Buddhism, talks and events – also has podcasts to download: **www.buddhistgeeks.com**

▶ Oxford Centre for Mindfulness, training, practice and teaching of mindfulness: **www.oxfordmindfulness.org**

▶ Bangor Centre for Mindfulness, research and practice, Wales: **www.bangor.ac.uk/mindfulness**

▶ The Barn, retreat centre, Devon: **www.sharphamtrust.org/ The-Barn-Retreat**

▶ Gaia House, retreat centre, Devon: **www.gaiahouse.co.uk**

▶ London/Bristol/Sheffield/Nottingham/Milton Keynes insight groups – see also: **http://gaiahouse.co.uk/resources/local-meditation-groups/** for lists of local groups

▶ Plum Village, retreat centre, France: **www.plumvillage.org**

▶ Moulin de Chaves, retreat centre, France: **www.moulindechaves.org**

▶ Spirit Rock, retreat centre, US: **www.spiritrock.org**

▶ Action for Happiness: **www.actionforhappiness.org**

▶ Free Mindfulness, loads of information and free to download guided mindfulness practices: **www.freemindfulness.org**

Index